The big GIANT DECISION... HOMESCHOOL!

Detailed Notes! Why We Did It! How You Can Do It!

by Penni Renee Pierce

plus A RESOURCE GUIDE

OVER 400 Listings
Books, Curricula, Internet Sites!

Third Edition

Pennymark Publishing

2

The Big GIANT Decision...Homeschool!   By Penni Renee Pierce

First Edition(1996) - Penmar Press
Second Edition (2006)- Thunderbolt Book & Art Publishers ISBN 13: 978-0-9789343-0-9
ISBN 10: 0-9789343-0-X

Third Edition (2007)- Pennymark Publishing
ISBN 13: 978-0-9797725-0-4
ISBN 10: 0-9797725-0-8

All photographs by the Pierce Family.

Cover design by Penni Pierce
Original book layout by Charles Pierce & Penni Pierce
Second & Third Edition book layout by Penni Pierce

Special thanks to Jean Reed for permission to quote her husband, the late Donn Reed. (page 105)

Published in the United States of America by

Pennymark Publishing

www.pennymarkpublishing.com

The Big GIANT Decision...Homeschool! By Penni Renee Pierce

3

C1

TABLE OF CONTENTS

24.00 1/23/08 Amazon.com (24.00)

4

The Big GIANT Decision...Homeschool! By Penni Renee Pierce

TABLE OF CONTENTS *(continued)*

TABLE OF CONTENTS *(continued)*

WHY WE DID IT! HOW YOU CAN DO IT!

Listed Below: Detailed Notes Of Our Homeschool Experience

TABLE OF CONTENTS *(continued)*

7

The Big GIANT Decision...Homeschool! By Penni Renee Pierce

TABLE OF CONTENTS *(continued)*

E X T R A   S T U F F!

8

The Big GIANT Decision…Homeschool! By Penni Renee Pierce

<u>TABLE OF CONTENTS</u> *(continued)*

HOW TO USE THIS BOOK

THE RESOURCE GUIDE

This book is a compilation of detailed notes about our family's success with homeschool. This fall we will start our 14th year of homeschool! The third edition of ***The Big Giant Decision*** contains almost everything from the first and second editions. The lay out is a little different in hopes that the book will become more useful and convenient for the reader. The first part of the book is the actual ***Resource Guide***. It is in alphabetical order according to subject. This will enable you to look up things quickly. Also, it is very convenient to carry the ***Resource Guide*** with you to the library. I have found the public libraries to be a great source of help. When someone recommends a book to me, I then go to the library and bring the book home and see if it is actually something that will help me. I have also found many books this way and then purchased them later, as that particular book became a favorite and we wanted to use it more often in our home. I have also added notes to various sections of the ***Resource Guide*** that may help you with your homeschooling. For example, in the *Language* section under *Reading*, I wrote an *EXTRA* note about how I taught Briana and Kyla to read. In the *Music* section I wrote an *EXTRA* note about how we taught our children music and never spent a penny on lessons. So, along with the lists of books and materials, you may also want to *read* the ***Resource Guide***. Additions to the ***Resource Guide*** also include *Field Trips – Internet Style, Life Skills, Learning Disabilities, Special Needs, Music, Scholarships, and Support Groups*.

THE LAW

Also, within the ***Resource Guide***, you will find a page about the law. This will show you how to find out your state laws for homeschooling, plus the author's thoughts on obeying the law.

SUPPORT GROUPS

This section will help you to contact others in your state that homeschool.

GETTING STARTED CHECK LIST

Easy checklist to start homeschooling now!

WHY WE DID IT! HOW YOU CAN DO IT!

After the ***Resource Guide***, I placed the ***Why we did it! How you can do it!*** section of the book. This is where you will find detailed notes of our first year homeschooling. As

10

The Big GIANT Decision...Homeschool!   By Penni Renee Pierce

I write the third edition, we will be entering our 14th year of homeschool. Many things have happened since that first year and now 13 years later, I have added *Extra* notes throughout the book. I felt this would be helpful, as you will see the schedules and activities we are still doing, after 13 years, also I noted things I felt needed further explanation.

HOMESCHOOL GRADUATES ENTER COLLEGE

I have also included in the third edition, a section called ***The Homeschool Graduate Goes to College*** and ***The Graduated Homeschoolers' Commentary.*** This includes our experiences transitioning into college and some tips from our own homeschool graduates, plus a sample high school transcript!

ADDITIONAL INFORMATION

Also included are *A Father's Thoughts On Homeschool*, *Every Child's Dream* (a poem about mothers), *The Homeschool Guarantee,* the *M.D. Pierce Academy Homeschool Yearbook* and some funny anecdotes and quotes about education and homeschool.

11

The Big GIANT Decision...Homeschool!   By Penni Renee Pierce

FOREWORD

I am seriously wondering if I should be attempting to write a foreword to a book advocating "Homeschool".

Back in the 1930's and 40's when I was engaged in teaching and administration in the public schools, I was very much against homeschooling. I saw several unsuccessful attempts to carry out a schooling program in the home with the results of some very frustrated parents and some "unschooled" kids who hated the looks of any school book and who lacked the ability to happily and successfully relate with children their own age. I'm sure there were some successes, but I didn't see them.

Then came the almost forced trend toward unionization of the local, state and national professional education organizations. I could see the genuine concern for children descending to the attitude and goals of big labor. I was not against labor unions for "labor", but, in my opinion, unions were not for professional educators. That's when I went into industry as my life's work.

Now with the federally mandated rules and regulations and less and less local control of education, I can understand the demand of many parents for a genuine "children oriented" school atmosphere and real local control for their children. What can be more "local" than the home?

Fortunately, I have now seen some very successful "Homeschools", none more so than the one about which this book is written. Penni has pointed out many of the pitfalls and challenges involved in starting and continuing your own homeschool. If you're thinking about beginning homeschooling, this book can help you determine if you're the kind of person who can meet those challenges. The book is also a treasure trove of resources for the parent who's looking for materials to assist in teaching and to enrich the education environment in the home. For those parents who need a cheerleader, Penni has also pointed out the joy and satisfaction a real teacher gets when a child's face lights up as new ideas and understanding emerge. And that is worth a million.

If you are considering the possibility of homeschooling, a Homeschool might be just what you are hoping for and looking for and this book will help. If you are already in the thick of the process and an experienced parent/teacher, this book will be a valuable resource for you. I heartily recommend it.

-D.P. (Andy) Anderson
Former Public School Teacher and Principal

NOTE: Andy's first experience teaching was while he was still a college student. He taught Botany Lab classes to freshmen. He later became a high school science teacher and then the principal of that same school. When Andy and his family moved to Nevada, he worked in the public schools as a high school principal for approximately six years. Andy and his wife, Pearl, of 60 years, raised three boys. After leaving education, Andy was employed by the Atomic Energy Commission for the United States government.

12

The Big GIANT Decision...Homeschool!   By Penni Renee Pierce

ABOUT THE AUTHOR

Penni Renee Pierce was born in Oak Ridge, Tennessee. Her family later moved to Dallas, Texas where she met and married her husband, Mark Pierce in 1981. They have five children.   Penni opted to homeschool her children in 1994 and has never looked back. Penni has spent many hours on the phone and sitting at her dining room table helping mothers and fathers decide if homeschooling was right for them. She wrote The Big GIANT Decision... Homeschool! as a result of keeping detailed notes while homeschooling her first year. Now, Penni has three graduated homeschoolers and two children still at home. The Big Giant Decision offers insight into the transition from homeschool to college and gives comments and suggestions from Penni's real life experiences and from her own homeschool graduates! Penni and Mark have always lived in the city until recently. They now enjoy living on the plains of North Texas in their 100 year old home, which is currently being restored.

13

The Big GIANT Decision...Homeschool!   By Penni Renee Pierce

DEDICATION

I dedicate this book to my husband.
I love him.
He gives constant, unswerving devotion,
And is a loving father.

And, of course, to my children Mark, Rachel, Tahnee, Briana and Kyla
Who make life sweeter than I could imagine.
And I want them to know...
Anything is possible and learning never ends!!!

Also, there is an extraordinary person that is a teacher among teachers. She has dedicated many years of her life to helping children. She was the one who went the extra mile; who stayed up late making a teaching event special; the one who worked until it was done; the one who was not satisfied with a half-hearted attempt. Her heart was at the center of every project. And everyone around her knew it. She expected much from her students. I happened to be one of her students, not one of the ones who sat at a desk in her classroom, but one of the ones who sat at the desk of life and observed her care and concern for others. There are many who have known her and she has touched their lives and affected them by her endeavors and encouragement. She is a teacher among teachers; in and out of the classroom and I respectfully and admiringly also dedicate this book to her, PEARL TAYLOR ANDERSON.

(Pearl substituted high school classes for approximately six years. She later taught elementary school full-time for two years and junior high for eight years.)

EXTRA NOTE: When I first started compiling The Big Giant Decision, Pearl and Andy read a rough copy of it and encouraged me a great deal. As I started the second edition of this book "Pearl-O" passed away. And while finishing up the second edition Pearl's husband, Andy, has since passed away. Andy wrote the **Foreword** for **The Big Giant Decision**. We will miss them so much!

14

The Big GIANT Decision...Homeschool!   By Penni Renee Pierce

PREFACE

It has always been a dream of mine to write a book. However, I never dreamed I would write a book about homeschool. This book "came to be" from keeping detailed notes of our first year homeschooling our children. When these notes were compiled, I knew it was a book. There are many parents that are honestly considering alternative education, whether it be private school or homeschool. This book is truly written from my heart about a subject close to my heart- my family. Maybe it will help you consider the alternative of homeschool. You will learn the details of our family's adventure after only one year of homeschool, with very satisfying results. *(With 13 years gone by, we have added EXTRA NOTES to the second and third editions)* This book also includes a *Resource Guide.* This guide will help you to know what is available for homeschoolers and how to order the materials you need.   As for the veteran homeschooler, this book may give you some fresh ideas and motivation to keep on track.

We are an ordinary family with ordinary kids who spill their milk, ride their bikes, skin their knees, wish math had never been invented, and have to be told again and again to do their chores. We live in the suburbs, in a small, three-bedroom home. I admit, our children are neither "gifted" nor "attention deficit" and neither are their parents! We just happen to homeschool our children instead of public school them. Parents CAN successfully homeschool their children. And they do not need an out-of-the-ordinary kid or situation to do it. Parents just have to figure out if it is right for themselves and their family.

Please take this book with its ideas and activities as suggestions, for that is what they are, because all families have to find their own way on their homeschool adventure. I hope *The Big Giant Decision* will be a piece of the map for your journey.

EXTRA NOTE: We will be starting our 14ᵗʰ year of homeschooling since writing the first edition of The Big Giant Decision. Meanwhile, we have moved out of the city to a small town, still in Texas, of course. Our town has a population of 245 people. We live in a 100 year old home on about an acre. We have puppies, kittens and chickens! The kids love it. Our two oldest, Mark and Rachel were married last summer about 60 days apart! We are thrilled to have a new son and daughter-in-law added to our family.

15

The Big GIANT Decision...Homeschool!   By Penni Renee Pierce

The
RESOURCE
GUIDE

Children will educate themselves under the right conditions.
-Helen Keller

ART
Art Books, Curricula, Internet Sites
(Includes Art History and Arts & Crafts)

Art Curriculum by How Great Thou Art Publications
1-800-982-3729
www.howgreatthouart.com
-A great art program
-Very pleasant internet site
-Age 3 thru Adult

Art For Children by Ernest Raboff
-This is a series of art books featuring 16 different artists. They are:

Renoir	Van Gogh
DaVinci	Michelangelo
Rembrandt	Raphael
Picasso	Chagall
Gauguin	Matisse
Velasquez	Remington
Klee	Durer
Rousseau	Toulouse-Lautrec

-Great text
-Each book has about 15 full-color reproductions
-These books are normally about $8.00 a piece, but I found several of them at our discount book store for $2.98 each.
-This series was highly recommended to me by several people that homeschool. So if you want to do art history, this is a good start.

Come Look With Me by Gladys S. Blizzard
- This is for younger children, however could be adapted for older children also.
-This book shows beautiful paintings and gives questions to ask your child.
-The questions in this book could also be a start for creative writing papers with older children.

17

The Big GIANT Decision...Homeschool!   By Penni Renee Pierce

Crafts From The Past (series)
The Egyptians
The Greeks
The Romans
by Gillian Chapman
-We have really enjoyed these.
-Many ideas on how to make jewelry, pictures, arts and crafts and models

Good Earth Arts by Ann F. Kohl & Cindy Gainer
-Arts and crafts from nature and recyclables
-Great ideas!

Horses and Ponies (Draw Science Series)
by Susan Coleridge   Illustrations by Michelle Maltseff
-Learn to draw all different kinds of horses with their bodies and heads at different angles
-My girls really liked how this book helped them draw horses with more realistic features.

I Can Draw   "Animals"
by Walter Foster
-This is for the beginning artist.

Kids Art
www.kidsart.com
-Hands-on art education for home and school
-Art supplies
-Art Teaching books
-Art lesson plans
-Some free lesson plans
-This site has everything for art!

The Kid's Encyclopedia of Things To Make and Do
by Richard Michael Rasmussen & Ronda Lea Rasmussen
-Lots of ideas
-All ages

18

The Big GIANT Decision…Homeschool!   By Penni Renee Pierce

Places In Art by Anthea Peppin (by Millbrook Press)
-This is a series: ***Nature In Art, People in Art, Stories in Art***
-This is for kids of all ages.
-There is a famous painting with some history and then ideas on creating your own artwork.
-I like this.

Sketching Outdoors in Summer
by Jim Arnosky
-This is for older children and the more serious artist.

Teaching Drawing Skills
www.everydayart.com
-Curriculum plans for teaching and home schoolers
-All the lessons are free right there on the site!

Teaching Ideas
www.teachingideas.co.uk
-click "art"
-Lots of submitted ideas
-Art displays
-Art links

The Big GIANT Decision...Homeschool!   By Penni Renee Pierce

19

CATALOGS AND MATERIALS
Homeschool Companies, Internet Sites

A Beka Book
1-800-874-3592 US & Canada
850-479-6585 International
www.abeka.org

Academic Superstore
1-800-392-6427
www.HC.AcademicSuperstore.com
-Discounts for homeschoolers
-Hardware and software, lots!!

Alpha Omega Publications
1-800-622-3070
www.aop.com
-Web store

The Always Incomplete Resource Guide and Catalog
(See "Lifetime Books and Gifts" in this guide)
www.lifetimebooksandgifts.com
-available online only

At Last! A Reading Method For Every Child!
By Mary F. Pecci, M.A., Reading Specialist
415-391-8579
970-493-3793
www.onlinereadingteacher.com
-Pecci reading method
-"The reading method that breaks the mold"
-Intensive phonics and literature-based readers
-Video workshops

Bluestocking Press
1-800-959-8586
www.bluestockingpress.com
-Publisher of Uncle Eric Books by Richard J. Maybury
-"Hard to find museum store specialties"

20

The Big GIANT Decision…Homeschool! By Penni Renee Pierce

-Historical Documents
-Books, Music, Toys, Primary Sources

Bob Jones University Press
1-800-482-2889 Order Line
716-532-1888
www.pennywiselearning.com
-"The Best in Homeschooling…Made Affordable!"
-They sell their own curricula.
-This is also a school.

The Book Peddler
440-284-6654
www.bookpeddler.us/
-Great resource for all kinds of books.
-Lots of stuff!!
-Homeschooling materials

Brook Farm Books
(See *The Home School Book Source* listed in this section)

Cadron Creek Christian Curriculum
505-534-1496
www.CadronCreek.com
-The Prairie Primer is a literature-based unit study, utilizing the *Little House on the Prairie* Series.
-For grades 3 – 6
-Units also for grades 4-8
-Units for Jr. High and High School
-"Victorian" Era, "Pioneer" Era, "Narnian" Era

Calliope Books
-Other homeschool bookstores carry these products (There is not a web site as of yet. There is a www.calliope.com site under construction as I write this second edition.).
- Foreign language materials
- Tapes, books, readers, grammar books
- Just about any language you could think of such as, Vietnamese, Arabic, Polish, Welsh, Hebrew and many others

The Big GIANT Decision...Homeschool! By Penni Renee Pierce

21

CER Curriculum
435-586-8591
www.cerlink.com
-Pre-school thru college prep
-Offers curriculum sets
-Offers testing to see how your children are doing

www.cheec.com
-The address is the name of their site.
-Look through and click "homeschool"
-Listings for homeschool companies
-Educational materials including learning disability software

Chinaberry Books
www.chinaberry.com
1-800-776-2242 to order
1-888-481-6744 questions
-Online bookstore
- I love this catalog of books.
- I take it to the library with me and check out many of the books there first, then I will buy the ones I want.
- I have found some wonderful treasures through this catalog.

Christian Book Distributors
Homeschool Resources Catalog
1-800-247-4784
www.christianbook.com

Cobblestone Publishing Company
1-800-821-0115
www.cobblestonepub.com
-Social Studies, Science, English Language Arts
-Magazines
-Books
-Homeschool teaching products

College Without Compromise by Scott & Kris Wightman
"An Encouraging Guide to Starting Early, Finishing Economically, and Protecting Your Homeschool Vision"

22

The Big GIANT Decision...Homeschool! By Penni Renee Pierce

The Cornerstone Curriculum Project
(214) 235-5149
www.CornerstoneCurriculum.com
(family owned business)
-Owned by David and Shirley Quine
-David Wrote the math curriculum "Making Math Meaningful".
-Homeschool curriculum
-Convention information and more!

The Critical Thinking Company
1-800-458-4849
www.criticalthinking.com
-Builds thinking skills
-Books and software for science, history and math and more!
-PreK- grade 12
-"Problem-solving skills for life"

Design-A-Study
1-800-965-2719
302-998-3889
www.designastudy.com
-Read about Kathryn Stout, a public school teacher who homeschooled her children and put this curricula together.
-Mission Statement: "Design-A-Study is committed to offering affordable curricula and resources that allow parents and educators the flexibility necessary to meet individual learning needs."
-Homeschool forum
-Teaching help

Discount Homeschool Supplies
828-632-9114
www.dhss.com

Friendship House
1-800-791-9876
www.friendshiphouse.com
-Musical gifts, awards & teaching aids
-Wonderful teaching tools and incentives!
-Reproducibles

23

The Big GIANT Decision...Homeschool!   By Penni Renee Pierce

God's World Book Club
1-800-951-2665
www.gwbc.com

Great Homeschool Books
www.greathomeschoolbooks.com
-New & used homeschool books

Green Leaf Press Catalog
 (615)449-1617
www.greenleafpress.com
-Many, many books for homeschoolers with critiques
-Well known for their history study guides
-I especially love their Ancient Egypt, Ancient Greece & Ancient Rome history materials.

Home Again
www.home-again.com
-Click "homeschooling"
-A resource site with links
-Teaching supplies
-Waldorf

The Home Computer Market
P.O. Box 385377
Bloomington, Minnesota 55435
(612)844-0462
www.homecomputermarket.com
-They sell educational software for homeschoolers.
-They warn against unwholesome software.
-Call or write for a catalog with very informative critiques.

Home-ed-press
www.home-ed-press.com
-Great resource site
-Online schools

24

The Big GIANT Decision...Homeschool!   By Penni Renee Pierce

The Home School Book Source** by Donn Reed
Brook Farm Books
Toll Free: 1-877-375-4680
www.brookfarmbooks.com
-I really enjoyed Donn's book!
-Well worth the money!
-Lots of products and companies listed that are not in some of the other catalogs!
-I admire Donn for producing a book to help others learn the resources available.
-His outlook on homeschool is very candid.
-After Donn passed away his wife, Jean, worked very hard on a second edition of this book. It has doubled in size, about 400+ pages!

Homeschool Bookworm
256-825-5400
www.homeschoolbookworm.com
-New and used curriculum

Homeschool Favourites
www.homeschoolfavourites.com
-Offers literature-based curriculum
-Very good site
-Lots of books, articles, events.
-Uses Charlotte Mason's philosophy which says, "The only real education appears to be that children should read worthy books- many worthy books."

John Holt-
Growing Without School
www.holtgws.com
-Learn about John Holt.
-John Holt is considered the original homeschool advocate.
-Learn about "unschooling".
-Order his book "The Underachieving School" which is back in print after 30 years.

Jostens
www.jostens.com
-Homeschool graduation accessories
-Create your own high school rings, yearbooks, diplomas, sports gear

25

The Big GIANT Decision...Homeschool!   By Penni Renee Pierce

Joy of Learning
1-800-490-4430
www.joyoflearning.com
-Online homeschool consultant
-Software
-Curricula, resources, classroom supplies
-Arts and crafts
-Used curriculum for sale

Kid Advance Montessori Store (Look under Montessori)

Lifetime Books and Gifts**
1-800-377-0390 Orders only
863-676-6311 Questions
www.lifetimebooksandgifts.com
-Look for "The Always Incomplete Resource Guide and Catalog" by Bob and Tina Farewell.
-This catalog is now available online only.
-This is a catalog for you to order homeschool materials, but also Bob and Tina and their staff critique the things they sell.
-A valuable resource
-If you plan to homeschool, get this catalog!

Love To Learn
1-801-798-1034 Questions & Orders
1-888-771-1034 Orders
www.lovetolearn.net
-I love this company.
-This is a homeschool store!
-Quality homeschooling materials
-The critiques this family has put together on their products are invaluable.
-They have written some of their own curricula, such as "Happy Phonics".

Kid Advance Montessori Store (sorry I put this out of alphabetical order to keep it with the Montessori listings)
www.kidadvance.com
-Great store for Montessori products

26

The Big GIANT Decision...Homeschool!   By Penni Renee Pierce

Montessori Homeschooling

www.montessori.edu/homeschooling.html

-This is a great site to find out about Montessori and how to use it with homeschooling.

Montessori Software

"Your Own Private Montessori Tutor. Always Patient – Always Present"

1-800-791-1388

www.mecssoftware.com/home.htm

-I love the Montessori method of teaching!! I used a lot of these ideas when my children were very young.

-This site has materials for ages 2 – 12 years.

www.puremontessori.com

-Great information site!

Moody Science Video Collection

www.moodyvideo.org

-A collection of science videos that do not leave God out of the picture.

My Father's World

573-426-4600

www.mfwbooks.com

-The thing that interested me the most about this company is their multi-age unit studies.

-Also, their family story is very interesting!

-Materials for preschool thru grade 8

National Center for Constitutional Studies

1-800-388-4512

www.nccs.net

-A very patriotic site!

-Constitution study courses

-Wonderful history books, paintings and documents

Pioneer Drama Service, Inc.

"Touching Lives Through Theatre"

1-800-796-7280

www.pioneerdrama.com

-Great to use in teaching reading and/or public speaking.

-Many of these plays could be used by support groups.
-Well done internet site

Sing and Learn
"Make Learning Fun Through Music"
1-800-460-1973
www.singnlearn.com
-Learn Math, Science, History, Foreign Languages and Scriptures with music

Timberdoodle Company
"Meeting the needs of homeschoolers since 1985"
www.timberdoodle.com
-Homeschool bookstore!

Waldorf Answers
www.waldorfanswers.org
-If you would like to know about Waldorf and their philosophies, this is a very good site.
-I have not used Waldorf, but I have friends that really like it. Homeschool parents can read many different ideas and glean from it the things they would like to use in their homeschool.

The Weaver Curriculum
(Listed below are the sites that will help you get to know the Weaver Curriculum.)
- www.TheJubileeAcademy.org
- www.The-Home-Schooler.com
- www.AGDistribution.com
- www.info.com/TheWeaverCurriculum

The Well-Trained Mind
A Guide to Classical Education at Home by Jessie Wise and Susan Wise Bauer
www.welltrainedmind.com
-This was suggested by a homeschooling friend.
-The site is very nice and makes you want to read everything about it!

**The catalogs that I highly recommend to help you get started.

COMPUTERS & INTERNET
The Author's Thoughts

Wrong Address

One day I was going to a website for which I thought I knew the address. I typed in one wrong letter and a pornography site came up. I was so appalled and outraged, I couldn't even figure out how to get it off the screen quick enough. Holding one arm over the screen and clicking with the other hand I finally came to my senses and removed it!!!!

A Wonderful & Dangerous Tool!

It was hard to write this section of the book, because I have mixed feelings about the internet. I feel there have been good things accomplished because of the internet, but there are also some people who have their own agendas and will complete their agenda at all costs- even at the cost of our children. I believe the internet to be a wonderful and dangerous tool! I have yet to see a "fool-proof" safety software for the internet. So, the best way to monitor the internet is to research and find a safety software and use it, talk with your children about the dangers of the internet and be nearby when the internet is in use. You may want to keep your computer in a high traffic part of your home instead of in a bedroom.

What To Recommend?

Also, I had a hard time deciding if I should recommend websites or not, because they change so much. But, in my search I found some wonderful things and great information. If I recommend a website, that doesn't necessarily mean I think the whole site is wonderful, it just means I feel that it would be worth your time to look at it, if it fits your curriculum or interests. I was going to list some computer self-help books, but they will be outdated the second I start to type their title!!! So I suggest finding that kind of help at a discount bookstore or over the internet.

Software Savvy

Our children were born into the technological era. Computers are not scary to them. In fact, they adapt to them very naturally. At times, my husband and I have to ask them how to "import" something OR where is the tool for this? They usually know! We are also encouraging them to learn software. Any software they learn will help them understand new software and will benefit them later when applying for jobs. Our daughter Briana, at 14, spent over 200 hours on a project learning a movie making software and producing a wedding video for her sister, Rachel. She is now working

29

The Big GIANT Decision...Homeschool!   By Penni Renee Pierce

with a different movie making software and everything she learned from the original software has helped her and has been a great asset as she builds upon previous learning.

She is beginning work on her brother's wedding video now. You would never know that a "kid" put these videos together. They are extremely professional and artistic. She is very talented.

FIELD TRIPS – *INTERNET STYLE*
Virtual Field Trip Sites

Crow Canyon Archaeological Center
www.crowcanyon.org

Education Planet
www.educationplanet.com
-Lists of virtual field trips

Electronic Field Trips
www.efieldtrips.org
-National points of interest

Exploratorium Science Museum
www.exploratorium.edu
-Interactive exhibits
-Ideas & activities

Homefires
The Journal of Homeschooling Online
www.homefires.com
-List of virtual field trips

Internet 4 Classrooms
www.internet4classrooms.com
-All about virtual field trips with links

Smithsonian Institute
www.si.edu
-Virtual Smithsonian Museum
-Visit the Smithsonian without leaving your home!! With sound!

Tramline
www.field-guides.com
-This is a site with lists of virtual field trips.

Volcano World Virtual Field Trips
www.volcano.und.edu

31

The Big GIANT Decision...Homeschool!   By Penni Renee Pierce

White House Tours for kids

www.whitehouse.gov

-You can tour the rooms of the White House!

-Learn history

-Write to the White House

32

The Big GIANT Decision...Homeschool! By Penni Renee Pierce

GEOGRAPHY
Books, Materials, Curricula

Beautiful Feet Books "Geography Through Literature"
1-800-889-1978 Orders
314-721-5238 Questions
www.bfbooks.com
-Can be used for grades K – 12
-They sell Rea & Rebecca Berg's *History Through Literature Study Guides*.
-I really enjoyed viewing the samples of this material. It is very well done and takes the student through various exercises to encourage pondering and understanding of the time period being studied.

A Child's Geography of the World by V.M. Hillyer
-Highly recommended
-Out-of-print
-You may be able to find this by doing an internet book search. Some homeschooling companies will do a book search for you also.

Children Like Me by Barnabas & Anabel Kindersley
-This is a fun book with real pictures of children from all over the world.
-Each page is full of information about what the child wears, what they eat, where they live, how they live and more!
-This is a very fun way to study geography.
-Kyla, our youngest wanted to go to Russia after learning about Olia and Dasha, two darling little sisters from Russia.

Geography Matters
606-636-4678
www.geomatters.com
-I think this may be "the" geography site!!
-Everything you need!

Hands-On Geography
"Easy and Fun Activities for Exploring God's World"
by Maggie S. Hogan and Janice Baker
-Fun geography games and activities adaptable for all ages

Hewitt Homeschooling Resources
1-800-890-4097
360-835-8708

www.hewitthomeschooling.com
-United States Geography
-Elementary thru high school level materials
-This is a whole resource site, not just geography.

Homeschoolstore.com
www.homeschoolstore.com
-Grades 1 – 6
-Unit studies
-Map skills, geography, literature
-All subjects

Literature-Based Map Skills (Sniffen Court Books) by Maria Fleming
-Grades 1 - 3
-Uses story excerpts from favorite children's literature to gain mapping skills
-Teaches small sections of the United States at once, so when you finish the series you will have studied the entire United States.
-I purchased this at a teacher's store.

Maps and Globes by Jack Knowlton
-History of maps
-Map language

Maps and Mapping by Barbara Taylor
-Geography facts and experiments

Odyssey Atlasphere
-The globe that talks!
-Touch the atlasphere and it will tell you about that country.
-Comes with several games
-Great interactive way to learn geography
- www.home-school.com carries this product

Runkle Geograph
www.runklepub.com
-Order these products thru www.geomatters.com (606-636-4678)

34

The Big GIANT Decision...Homeschool! By Penni Renee Pierce

-Grades 6-12
-Physical geography, mapping

Words for the World by Christine Ege
-Introduces 8 countries and their languages and culture
-Book and cassette set
-Probably written for elementary age, but even my pre-teens enjoyed it.
-Of course, the library has many, many resources for any country you want to study, but this program is great for kids to hear the sound of the language and actually practice saying the words, too.
-This may not still be in print.
-Look on www.usedhomeschoolbooks.com

The Big GIANT Decision...Homeschool! By Penni Renee Pierce

35

HISTORY
Books We Love

ABC Book of Early Americana by Eric Sloane
-This is an ABC book for older children 7 - up
-Each page is a letter in the alphabet and many drawings of tools, antiquities and culture from early American history.

Book of Authentic Indian Life Crafts
by Oscar E. Norbeck
-Very good
-Library book

The Book of Indian Crafts and Indian Lore
by Julian Harris Salomon
-Good historical facts
-If you want authentic Indian crafts, this is good.
-Crafts, songs, languages
-Library book

The Blackfoot by Elizabeth Hahn
-Very good
-Library book
-We read this aloud.

A Child's History of Art* by V.M. Hillyer (out-of-print)
A Child's History of the World* by V.M. Hillyer (out-of-print)
-Look at book sales and half price book stores
-My friend found one and gave it to me!!
-Highly recommended!

A Child's Story of America by Michael J. McHugh
-Good overview of American History
-We purchased and read this aloud.

Colonial American Crafts "The Village" (a series) by Judith Hoffman Corwin
-For ages 8 - up
-Very effective to use with study of American history

36

The Big GIANT Decision...Homeschool!   By Penni Renee Pierce

Colonial Living by EdwinTunis
-Great resource

-Great drawings of authentic tools and homes from that era

Daniel Boone by Augusta Stevenson (The Childhood of Famous American Series)
-Excellent
-We read this aloud.
-Borrowed from a friend
-The kids absolutely loved this book and six months later still talked about Daniel Boone.
- I will be collecting this series now!

Early Health and Medicine by Bobbie Valman
-We read this aloud.
-Very interesting
-Library book
-This book is about what people throughout history believed about diseases and illnesses and cures.
-This is a great introduction to health today or anatomy.

Egypt: Activities & Projects by Josie Farnay and Claude Soleillant
-"All that you need to recreate the Egypt of King Tut, Cleopatra, and Nefertiti"
-Costumes, decorations, food, a game, hieroglyphics, crafts, and stories

Evangeline and the Acadians by Robert Tallant (A Landmark Book)
-Excellent, Excellent!
-I read this on my own and then shared the history of the Acadians with the kids. We then read Henry Wadsworth Longfellow's poem, "Evangeline", which is a historically accurate poem. Also, a great study of vocabulary!
-If you don't know about the Acadians, find out!!

From Barter to Banking (The story of money) by William W. Wade
-"America in the Making" Series
-I found this gem at the library.
-I will purchase as soon as I see it at a book sale.

Games of the American Indian by Gordon C. Baldwin
-Very good
-Tells how to play games with groups of kids

37

The Big GIANT Decision...Homeschool!   By Penni Renee Pierce

-Great fun
-Library book

-I picked games and stories out of this book to share with the kids.

If You Grew Up with Abraham Lincoln by Ann McGovern
-My children have really enjoyed these books.
-They answer many questions about the particular time period.
-More titles listed below:
If You Lived at the Time of Martin Luther King by Ellen Levine
If You Lived at the Time of the Civil War by Kay Moore
If You Lived at the Time of the Great San Francisco Earthquake by Ellen Levine
If You Lived in Colonial Times by Ann McGovern
If You Lived with the Sioux Indians by Ann McGovern
If You Sailed on the Mayflower by Ann McGovern
If You Traveled on the Underground Railroad by Ellen Levine
If You Traveled West in a Covered Wagon by Ellen Levine
If You Were There When They Signed the Constitution by Elizabeth Levy

The Iroquois by Craig A. and Katherine Doherty
-Very good
-Library book
-We read this aloud.

The Land of Fair Play by Christian Liberty Press
-Actually, a Civics course, but I will include it here in the history listings.
-Explains the founding of America and explains the constitution and our form of government.
-It is written for children, but I used it with even my high school kids and we had some wonderful conversations as a result of reading this aloud.
-I learned so much too!!
-You can also purchase this from **Love to Learn** catalog, see Catalogs section.

The Making of America *The Substance and Meaning of the Constitution* by Cleon Skousen
-A wonderful course in history and government
-Every adult and/or child should take this course
-Can be ordered from **Love to Learn** catalog, see Catalogs section.

38

The Big GIANT Decision...Homeschool!   By Penni Renee Pierce

N.C. Wyeth's Pilgrims by Robert San Souci, illustrated by N.C. Wyeth
-Excellent paintings!

-Good text for children learning about Pilgrims.

Paul Revere and the Minute Men
by Dorothy Canfield Fisher (An out-of-print Landmark Book)
-We read this aloud.
-Really enjoyed a view of the person, Paul Revere
-I collect Landmarks and find them at library sales or half price book stores.
-They are worth looking for.

Pyramid
Mill
Ship
Cathedral: The Story of Its Construction
City: A Story of Roman Planning and Construction
Underground
Castle
Unbuilding all of these written and illustrated by David Macaulay
-Wonderful history told
-Very easy to understand
-Very detailed pen-and-ink drawings make it come to life for the reader.

Sequoyah by Grant Foreman
-Good
-Biography
-Library book
-We read this aloud.

The Story of the Declaration of Independence
by Norman Richards (Cornerstones of Freedom series)
-We read this aloud.
-American History in story form
-I collect these and find them at half price book stores or book sales.

The Thirteen Colonies (A New True Book)
-Very good, simple overview of American History up to 1776
-Library book
-We read this aloud.

39

The Big GIANT Decision...Homeschool!   By Penni Renee Pierce

Thomas Jefferson Education (Teaching a New Generation of Leaders for the 21st Century) *A collection of speeches* by Oliver DeMille
www.gwc.edu
-This book was highly recommended.
-You can purchase from George Wythe College.

Uncle Eric Series by Richard J. Maybury
-I will list this series here in the history section, even though they include economics, finances and politics.
-Excellent books!
-Adults and children need to read this!
Book 1 *Uncle Eric Talks About Personal, Career and Financial Security* (Uncle Eric's Model introduced)
Book 2 *Whatever Happened to Penny Candy?* (The economic model explained.)
Book 3 *Whatever Happened to Justice?* (The legal model explained. Explores America's legal heritage.)
Book 4 *Are You Liberal? Conservative? Or Confused?* (Political Labels. What do they mean?)
Book 5 *Ancient Rome: How It Affects You Today*. (Mr. Maybury uses historical events to explain current events.)
Book 6 *Evaluating Books: What Would Thomas Jefferson Think About This?* (Learn how to identify the philosophical slant of most writers and media commentators on the subjects of law, economics and history.)
(The words in the parenthesis are by Bluestocking Press)
-You can order these from **Bluestocking Press**, see Catalogs section.

Wilma Mankiller by Jacki Thompson Rand
-Biography
-Library book
-We read this aloud.

The Young Reader's Companion to American History by John A. Garraty
-This has been a wonderful resource to quickly look up a person or an event in American History.
-My daughter Rachel even used it several times while taking a College History class!

*Books recommended by homeschooling friends

LANDMARKS

Landmark books are highly recommended. You can check them out at the library, but the libraries are gradually getting rid of these wonderful, old history books. The hardbacks are out-of-print, some have gradually come back into print maybe because of the high demand by homeschoolers.

JUST A THOUGHT – *Your study of History*

There are many ways to study history. As you figure out what you want to study, develop a basic outline of that time period. You may want to use several different sources about that era. It's fun to see different authors' views of the Revolutionary War, for example. Children will also begin to understand that there are many different sources of information and one history book's description doesn't necessarily mean that that is exactly how it happened.

The Big GIANT Decision...Homeschool!   By Penni Renee Pierce

41

HOW-TO, SELF-HELP & RESOURCE BOOKS
Homeschool Success & Motivation Books

Here are resource books and motivation books to help you!
(If there is something I do not agree with in a book, that is not to say you shouldn't get the book. I have listed here the ones that are worth the investment.)

Big Book of Home Learning* by Mary Pride (set of 4 books)
-List of materials
-Critiques homeschooling materials and curricula

Curriculum of Love by Morgan Simone Daleo

The Dan Riley School For a Girl: An Adventure in Home School by Dan Riley

Family Matters: Why Homeschooling Makes Sense by David Guterson

A Field Guide to Home Schooling *A Practical Guide For Parents* by Christine M. Field

For the Children's Sake: Foundations of Education for the Home and School
by Susan Schaeffer Macaulay
-This book is well written.
-If I could think of one phrase to describe this book it would be, "For the Children's Sake teaches parents to respect the child's individuality."
-I did not know who Charlotte Mason was until I read this. I wish I could have known her.
-I like Macaulay's idea that a child's attention, truthfulness, self-control and unselfishness can become a habit.

Homeschooling All The Way Through High School by Renee Mason
-I really enjoyed this book.
-The children also write some of it.
-I especially enjoy page 70 where the mother gives her opinion about socialization and the prom.
-It does include some resources in the back of the book.

The Homeschooling Book of Answers: *88 most important questions answered by homeschooling's most respected voices* compiled by Linda Dobson

42

The Big GIANT Decision...Homeschool!   By Penni Renee Pierce

The Homeschooling Father, The Key to Success and Sanity by Michael P. Farris
-My husband and I really enjoyed reading this view of the father's role in homeschooling.
-By the way, the author is a lawyer.

Homeschooling for Excellence by David and Micki
Colfax
-This is the homeschooling family that had three of their sons go to Harvard.
-This book really helped me to get started and gather up books and materials needed for our first year.
-Great book!

Homeschooling From Scratch: Simple Living, Super Learning by Mary Potter Kenyon

The Homeschooling Handbook: From Preschool to High School: A Parent's Guide
by Mary Griffith

Home School Manual by Theodore E. Wade
-Always being updated
-Many ideas!
-This is the book that gave me the idea of a Homeschool Open House.

Home School: Taking The First Step by Borg Hendrickson

How to Homeschool* by Gayle Graham

In Their Own Way *Discovering and Encouraging Your Child's Personal Learning Style*
by Thomas Armstrong, Ph.D.
-Interesting! To say the least!
-I lean toward being anti-test taking, except when being used as a tool to test a skill, so even though my mouth may have fallen open when reading the testing section, I am not surprised at the statistics! (You'll understand when you read it.)

Kids Who Start Ahead, Stay Ahead by Neil Harvey

Schooling At Home Parents, Kids and Learning from Mothering Magazine
edited by Anne Pedersen and Peggy O'Mara
-This book is divided into four parts: Thoughts on Learning, Legal Issue, Ways of Learning in the Home, Home Schooling Stories

The Big GIANT Decision...Homeschool! By Penni Renee Pierce

43

7 Laws of the Learner: How to Teach Almost Anything to Practically Anyone!*
by Bruce Wilkinson

Survivors Guide to Homeschooling
by Luanne Shackelford and Susan White
-Funny!
-I can relate!
-Do not agree with all of their philosophies.
The books listed above can be found at the library, your local bookstore, or from the companies listed in the **Homeschool Catalogs and Materials** section of this book.

*Books recommended by homeschooling friends.

44

The Big GIANT Decision...Homeschool!   By Penni Renee Pierce

PRESCHOOL SELF-HELP BOOKS

You have to do your own growing no matter how tall your grandfather was.
—Abraham Lincoln

The Busy Classroom by Patty Claycomb

Get Ready, Set, Grow! A Preplanned Calendar of Preschool Activities
by Eileen Morris and Stephanie Pereau Crilly

Home-Style Learning by Philip S. Morse and Lillian B. Brand

Nature for the Very Young by Marcia Bowden
-I found this at the library and then purchased it.
-I love this book!
-I thought that some of the concepts might be too advanced to present to my little 4 and 5 year olds, but they weren't. My girls responded and remembered the things that they learned from this book!!

Smart Times by Kent Garland Burtt

Teaching Kids to Love the Earth by Marina Lachecki Herman

Teaching Your Own Preschool Children by Kay Kuzma

300 Three Minute Games Quick and Easy Activities For 2-5 Year Olds
by Jackie Silberg

45

The Big GIANT Decision...Homeschool!   By Penni Renee Pierce

LANGUAGE
Creative Writing, Foreign Language, Grammar, Reading, Spelling, etc.

CREATIVE WRITING/WRITING SKILLS
Games for Writing by Peggy Kaye
-A book of games K-3
-Wonderful ideas to help kids write and overcome any fear of writing
-I wrote the ideas from this book on 3x5 cards and then we would just choose one and play the game!

God Made My World by Carol Ann Retzer
-A Beginners Book for Manuscript Writing
-Can be purchased from **Love to Learn** (see Catalog section)

Handwriting Without Tears by Jan Olsen
-I really like this.
-You need to have a little hand-held chalkboard for each child.
-Teaches children to write their letters
-Helps stop reversals such as "b" & "d"
-Purchase from **Love to Learn** (see Catalog section)

If You're Trying to Teach Kids How to Write... You've Gotta Have This Book!
by Marjorie Frank
-Let me tell you, if you are trying to teach your kids how to write, you've got to have this book!! I mean it! Lots and Lots of ideas!!!

Mega Skills by Dorothy Rich
-Great ideas! The writing umbrella, which Dorothy explains, helps kids to stay on the subject within a paragraph.

Write @ Home
www.WriteAtHome.com
-Writing curriculum for 6 – 12th grades
-Expert tutors
-Enroll online

Write Shop
www.writeshop.com
-Writing program for 7 – 12th grade

46

The Big GIANT Decision...Homeschool!   By Penni Renee Pierce

-Also some materials for grades 4 - 6
-Free sample write shop lesson

Writing Is A Blast by Kari Berge Brimhall
www.learningisablast.com
-This book is full of ideas for creative writing.
-Fantastic ideas!

FOREIGN LANGUAGE
Artes Latinae A Self-Teaching Latin Series
www.bolchazy.com
-For ages 10-up
-Latin on CD-Rom with Restored Classical and Ecclesiastical pronunciations

Cambridge Latin Course
www.cambridge.org
-Highly recommended by a homeschooling friend

English from the Roots Up by Joegil Lundquist
-We're using this system that teaches Latin roots.
-The kids are very excited about it.
-It will help improve reading, writing, spelling and SAT scores.
-For grades 2-12

Greek
www.opentexture.com
-Elementary Greek course for grade 2 up to adult

Latin & Logic
Classical Academic Press
www.ClassicalAcademicPress.com
-Latin and Logic materials for grades 3 and up
-I thought the name, *The Art of Argument,* was so appropriate for their junior high age logic curriculum!

The Learnables International Linguistics Corp.
www.learnables.com
-Highly recommended by many homeschoolers for learning a foreign language

47

The Big GIANT Decision...Homeschool!   By Penni Renee Pierce

Power-Glide Foreign Language Courses
www.power-glide.com
-Language courses for PreK - Adult
-You will be able to speak, write and read the language of your choice.
-My daughter studied the Power-Glide French. After she had studied French for about two years with this system, she went to a college French class. When the instructor heard her speak, she could not believe how well Tahnee's pronunciation was and wondered if she had already traveled to France!

Rosetta Stone
Language Learning Success
-30 languages available
-Learn to speak, read, write and listen

Words for the World by Christine Ege
-Introduce young children, PreK – age 10 to eight different languages
-Learn to say a few common sentences
-Listen to some scriptures read in that Language
-Can be purchased from **Lifetime Gifts and Books** (see Catalog Section)
-check www.usedhomeschoolbooks.com

GRAMMAR
Easy Grammar by Wanda C. Phillips
-I love the way she introduces prepositions first.
-Our 11 and 12-year-old do one to two sheets from this three to four times per week and check their own work. I don't feel that our 9-year-old needs this amount of grammar, yet.
-I will do this program with Briana and Kyla starting in their ninth grade year.

Daily Grams by Wanda C. Phillips
-These are books for all different ages.
-They are workbooks that provide a daily review of grammar.
-I would purchase these after you complete *Easy Grammar*.

The Latin Road to English Grammar
www.thelatinroad.com
-5th grade and up
-Earn 2 years of high school foreign language credit

48

The Big GIANT Decision...Homeschool!   By Penni Renee Pierce

-I am thinking of combining this with "English From the Roots Up" for our high school curriculum.

Learning Grammar Through Writing
by Sandra M. Bell and James I. Wheeler
-A book of grammar rules
-Use with *Learning Language Arts Through Literature* or another resource you enjoy

Learning Language Arts Through Literature
by Diane Welch and Susan Simpson
-This is a series of books for grades 1-12. The first few pages tell how to use the book. One book covers many areas for that grade level, such as spelling, grammar, using a phone book, doing a research paper, etc. Sometimes the student will be learning grammar from a passage from the Bible or a famous piece of literature.
-We have really enjoyed this series.
-This series has been updated and is more in depth.
-Those who have used the updated version have really enjoyed it.

Winston Grammar* by Paul Erwin
-Recommended by homeschool friends

READERS
A Beka Readers
-**Lifetime Books and Gifts** and also **Love to Learn** will sell used ones to you.
-I found many of these at discount book stores.
-They have wonderful stories on all different levels of reading

Beginning Steps to Reading
-A Mennonite publication
-We like this very simple beginner reader.
-Can be purchased from **Love to Learn** (see Catalog section)

It Happens on a Ranch (A Linguistic Reader)
-Published in 1965 by Harper and Row
-This is out of print, but you can find these old readers at book sales and garage sales sometimes.

Rookie Readers
-Good beginning reader books
-Especially enjoyed "Katie Did It", "Baby Animals", "If I were an Ant"

READING

I am always reading aloud to the kids. It may be history books, funny stories, novels, science or anything we need to learn or anything they want to learn. They choose their own personal reading books. I help them choose if they've finished a series and are trying to figure out, "what next?" Every now and then, have your children read aloud to you from their own personal book; even older children. It's fun to hear them read and you'll know if they're pronouncing words correctly.

EXTRA NOTE

HOW I TAUGHT BRIANA & KYLA TO READ

I wanted to add a note here about how I taught Briana & Kyla to read. Briana and Kyla are my little homeschool guinea pigs! Because Mark, Rachel and Tahnee had already learned to read and write in public school before we started homeschooling. First of all, I took a large poster board and glued 26 "library pockets" (you know those old paper pockets from library books) to the board. I found these pockets at a teacher's store. They had an assortment of bright colors. Each pocket represented a letter in the alphabet and then I had cards with pictures that could be placed in the pockets according to what letter the picture began with, for example a picture of a lion goes in the "L" pocket. Also, I made index cards with upper and lower case letters so they could match the letters by putting them in the correct pockets. We practiced and practiced saying the sounds of the letters. I would put pieces of construction paper on the ground with a different letter on each piece and then I would say a word. They had to go stand on the letter with which the word begins. They loved this. Also, one day I put some letters on the floor and then around the house to find things that started with those letters. I bought Diane Hopkins, "Happy Phonics" from www.lovetolearn.com. We used the phonics games from that and any other phonics idea books I could get my hands on. When the girls learned all of the sounds of the alphabet, then they would be able to read the Bob Books series. Now that they could make the sounds of all the letters, these books were easy to sound out. For example, one sentence might read "Matt sat on Sam". Each page has a

50

The Big GIANT Decision...Homeschool!   By Penni Renee Pierce

sentence like this, so they could successfully read the whole book themselves. The books gradually add new words and new sounds. It is fun to see their faces when they can read a "whole" book!! (the books are only about 5 or 6 pages long) After Bob Books we went to any beginning readers or "I Can Read" books. The girls progressed beautifully. Along with learning the sounds of the letters, we also integrated writing all of the letters. Reading and writing go hand in hand and should be taught together, I feel. Writing is basically learning to copy symbols. And if they are copying the letters as they are learning their sounds, it helps. Some children might not be interested in the writing aspect of it as quickly as they are interested in letter recognition. Just be patient, they will soon put two and two together.

Books Children Love, A Guide to the Best Children's Literature by Elizabeth Wilson
-Wonderful critiques of children's literature
-I use this all the time.

Bring the Classics to Life (series)
  ### Little Women designed by Philip J. Solimene
Published by Edcon
-You read a small section of the story, answer questions and look at new vocabulary.
-I like doing this one first, because my little girls are very familiar with the story line from the movie, so it makes it very fun for them.
-I purchased this at a teacher's store.
-There are many books in the series.
www.edconpublishing.com

Children and Family Classics
Newport Publishers
www.audiobookclassics.com
-Classics on tape
-Dramatized, sound effects and original music

Explode the Code
-A step by step workbook-style approach to reading and writing
-My kids really enjoyed this program.
-This program really reinforces the phonics.
-The kids love finishing a book and getting their new book.
-You can order this from **Love to Learn** (see Catalog section)

51

The Big GIANT Decision...Homeschool!   By Penni Renee Pierce

EyeOpeners! *How to Choose and Use Children's Books About Real People, Places, and Things* by Beverly Kobrin

Five In A Row* by Jane Claire Lambert
-Read a classic, then do Social Studies, Language Arts, Art, Math and Science based on great literature.

Get Ready To Read by Toni S. Gould (also see *30+ Games To Get Ready to Read* by the same author)

Go Phonics
www.gophonics.com
-K – 2^(nd) grade reading program
-For the gifted or struggling child
-Effective for dyslexia also

99 Ways To Get Kids To Love Reading *and 100 Books They'll Love* by Mary Leonhardt
-Quick tips for preK - teens
-A section on reading disabilities
-Good advice

The Phonics Road to Spelling and Reading
www.thephonicsroad.com
-K – 4^(th) grade curriculum
-DVD presentation

Prairie Primer using Little House on the Prairie series* by Margie Gray
-Unit study; science, social studies, history, writing, etc. based on series

The Read Aloud Handbook by Jim Trelease
-This book is another guide to books children enjoy.

Reading for the Love of It, Best Books for Young Readers by Michele Landsberg
-This book has a guide to more than 400 great children's books.
-Do not agree with some of the suggested books for the 13+ age group, but most suggestions are great!

52

The Big GIANT Decision...Homeschool! By Penni Renee Pierce

Teach America To Read and Spell by Frank C. Rogers
-I love this Direct Phonics Reading Program.
-It will also help your children to be better spellers.
-Can be purchased from **Love to Learn** (see Catalog section)

Teach Your Child To Read In 100 Easy Lessons by Siegfried Engelmann
-Can be purchased from **Love to Learn** (see Catalog section)
-I found mine at a discount book store.

30+Games to Get Ready to Read by Toni S. Gould
-Fun games to help your child reinforce phonics.

Total Language Plus
www.totallanguageplus.com
-Language Arts program for grade 3 -12
-Studies cover spelling, vocabulary, comprehension, listening, grammar and punctuation, analytical and critical thinking, writing and field trips/projects
-Limited teacher preparation

SPELLING

We have taken words from our scripture reading, history or personal reading. The kids would write these words. We would use them orally and written in sentences. We had spelling tests weekly or bi-weekly. In the last couple of years, I have mostly corrected spelling through the kids creative writing papers.

Building Spelling Skills by Christian Liberty Press
-Purchase from **Love to Learn** in the Catalog Section
-I like this because it uses lists with common suffixes and prefixes.
-It especially was nice to use after we had finished ***English From the Roots Up*** (A Latin Program purchased from **Lifetime Gifts and Books**, see Catalog Section).

*Books recommended by homeschooling friends.

The Big GIANT Decision...Homeschool!   By Penni Renee Pierce

53

THE LAW
Choice and Accountability

It is important for you to know the homeschooling laws for your state. You can contact The Home School Legal Defense Association (HSLDA) for information:

>Home School Legal Defense Association
>P.O. Box 159
>Paeonian Springs, Virginia 22129
>(540)338-5600
>www.hslda.org
>info@hslda.org

What Are The Laws?

The HSLDA website is a huge resource of information. They answer so many questions about homeschooling. I highly recommend going to this site and educating yourself about homeschool. You may want to become a HSLDA member. You will need to become very organized with homeschooling and keep very good records in order to be protected by HSLDA. Also, read their "frequently asked questions" section to help you understand what they do. Also, they have a "support group" part of their site where you will just click the state and a list of support groups will come up. This is very helpful, especially when you are starting homeschool or relocating to another state!!!!

When I contacted the Home School Legal Defense Association, they were very courteous and helpful. All your questions will be answered from reading their site, but if not you can call them. They do not have an 800 number in order to help cut down on their expenses. But, they will be glad to talk with you and answer any additional questions you have.

When we first started homeschool thirteen years ago, I tried to find the homeschooling laws for Texas at our local library. I had two librarians helping me. We were stumped or stupid, I'm not sure which! One of the librarians contacted our local legal library. This library also had a hard time figuring out what the laws were for homeschooling. You may have better luck at your local library or courthouse. If you attempt this, look under "Compulsary Attendance" or "School Attendance". If you understand legal jargon, you may be able to decipher the pages. Or if you go to the HSLDA site and click "In your State", you will be able to find the laws for your state. It is set up similar to the support group area of their site.

54

The Big GIANT Decision...Homeschool!   By Penni Renee Pierce

Choice and Accountability

Families have many choices concerning the education of their children. Whether they are public schooled, private schooled, homeschooled, tutored or whatever the case may be. It is important to remember that having the choice in the first place, is a blessing. I spoke with a mother from Italy who told me that homeschooling is not legal there and not only that, but her family and those in her social circle expect mothers to put their child in some kind of preschool (daycare) practically from the time they can walk. This really was upsetting to her because she wanted to be with her baby and not put him in the arms of someone else for the day. She was treated as if she were not making good choices for her child. Hopefully, as she sticks with her ideas and feelings about holding and caring for her own child, others will see the difference and maybe it will become the norm as it once was. Maybe one day she will have the freedom she longs for to enable her to homeschool.

In the United States, all states have different laws for homeschooling. We, as parents, are responsible for finding out what those laws are and abiding by them. Then, if we dislike the law, we have the privilege of helping to change it. The choices and freedoms that we enjoy are God-given. And with this gift comes accountability. Once we do choose how we will educate our children, then we need to account for our actions. We need to be diligent and responsible. I don't think we need to be tyrants, but we need to carry out our plan jointly with our children, listening to their input. Ultimately, the responsibility is ours and our child's; both, being prepared to account for his or her actions. The act of choosing is a blessing, as also is accounting for what we do. Choosing gives us a wonderful feeling of freedom and accounting for our actions shows us our own weaknesses and helps us to do better.

When I was first doing my research on homeschooling the year before we started, I was amazed at all the people who had homeschooled many years before I had decided to do it. They had been so diligent in doing something they really believed was, not only their choice, but the right decision for their children's education. I was so inspired by their efforts that I wrote this small tribute to them. *A Tribute to Homeschoolers...*

55

The Big GIANT Decision...Homeschool!   By Penni Renee Pierce

A Tribute to Homeschoolers...

There are so many who came before us, choosing to educate their children at home.
I'm speaking of the ones who chose homeschool, when the laws were not so generous,
But deeply believed in educating their own children;
The ones who felt that it should be a parent's right to choose.
The ones who helped change laws and make a point.
These are the ones I admire.
For, when our family chose homeschool, the laws were more favorable.
Our "fight" was far smoother than theirs.
I admire them and thank them, whoever they are, for making our homeschool transition painless.

We are now going forward on this homeschooling journey.
Hoping that we might help others along the way,
Making their choice a little less painful.
Hopefully, being good examples and helping to "right" some of the misunderstood Ideas about homeschoolers and their families.
We cannot speak for everyone, but we surely can be responsible for our own actions and the way we live our lives.

Thank you, homeschoolers today and of the past
For battling for a right, which you believe is yours.
Because of you, we now enjoy a wonderful educational experience with our children.

And our adventure continues...

-Penni Renee' Pierce

56

The Big GIANT Decision...Homeschool! By Penni Renee Pierce

LIFE SKILLS
Cooking, Money, Pets, Sewing, Special Needs, etc.

COMMUNICATION, EMPLOYMENT, ENTREPRENEURS, FIRST AID, MONEY SKILLS, etc.

The Lemonade Stand *A Guide to Encouraging the Entrepreneur in Your Child* by Emmanuel Modu
-Very helpful

Life Skills Curriculum
www.philliproy.com
-The curriculum includes many skills, some of which are: communication, self-control, decision making, reading ads, how to manage money, employment skills, ATM, Bank statements, checking accounts, credit cards, etc.

Life Skills for Children: Equipping Your Child For the Real World by Christine Field
-This book has everything about teaching life skills!

Money Instructor
www.moneyinstructor.com
-Lessons on checking accounts and checkbooks
-The lessons are right on the site
-You can even print out "practice" checks and check account ledgers!
-Lessons on earning & spending, basic money skills, saving & investing, careers & business
-I highly recommend teaching this especially in the high school years!

The Official Kid's Survival Kit *How To Do Things On Your Own* by Elaine Chaback and Pat Fortunato
-Includes everything from accidents, babysitting, blackouts, first aid, safety and much more
-A book that may help you to start a conversation with your children about many different things

COOKING
www.cookingwithkids.com

www.familyfun.com

The Big GIANT Decision...Homeschool!   By Penni Renee Pierce

57

www.foodnetwork.com

www.kidsrcooking.com

www.KidsThatCook.com

Learn to Cook
www.cooking101.abccook.com
-Cooking class DVD's
-For older children and adults who are really interested in cooking.

www.preparedpantry.com

DRIVING
Driver Ed In A Box
www.driveredinabox.com
-Definitely a needed life skill!!
-All I can say is good luck, parents!

PETS
The Country Vet's Book of Home Remedies for Dogs
by Consumer Guide editors

www.Crate-Training.com

Crate Training Your Dog by Pat Storer

Dog Grooming for Dummies
by Margaret H. Bonham

www.dogs.about.com

How to Housebreak Your Dog in Seven Days
by Shirlee Kalstone

Kids Training Puppies in 5 Minutes
by JoAnn Dahan

www.perfectpaws.com

58

The Big GIANT Decision...Homeschool!   By Penni Renee Pierce

www.petplace.com

www.wonderpuppy.net

You and Your Puppy: Training and Health Care for Your Puppy's First Year
By James Debitetto & Sarah Hodgson

EXTRA PET NOTES: I would like to tell you about our story with pets. I feel that teaching a child to take care of a living creature is definitely a life skill and one that should not be taken lightly! It is very important to teach children to treat animals with patience and kindness. So, with that being said, we have had fish, hamsters, parakeets, kittens, puppies, and chickens (we do name our chickens!!) Our most recent experience has been a very positive one. First of all, our two youngest daughters did a lot of research on the internet and from books to learn about dogs. After much deliberation, counseling (for the parents, Hee!), compromising and let's not forget, begging; we told our daughters that they could have a small dog each. (The "wanting and wishing" went on for several years, but we finally said yes around age 11 & 13 which was a perfect age, I feel.) Kyla, our youngest was mesmerized with dog books. She would look at them for hours when she was very young and later on at around age 8 she would read these <u>huge</u> dog books and tell us everything about dogs. She knew everything about dogs, even if they were good with children or not!!! It took her about three years to talk us in to it!! After a great amount of study, the girls decided on the Shih-tzu. These particular dogs can be very expensive, so we needed to find some that were not registered. Once we said "yes", to having a dog, Briana went on the internet and found some unregistered Shih-tzu's within a few minutes. We drove 2 ½ hours and they picked out a tiny newborn Shih-tzu puppy. During the next six weeks we had to wait for our puppies to be weaned. During this time, we read about four books on house training, crate training, trick training, and shih-tzu puppy history!! It was so fun! I took Kyla and Briana to the store and we got all the supplies they would need including a small baby playpen to keep the puppies in so that we would not step on them. Briana and Kyla were very excited, so the next few weeks seemed to drag on forever. Finally the day came, we drove the 2 ½ hours again to the lady's house. She knew we were coming and when we got there she was standing at the gate with the cutest, fluffy, shih-tzu puppies I had ever seen. Since six weeks had passed the little newborn pups had grown and had soft fluffy fur. Briana and Kyla could hardly speak. All you heard was Ohhhh!!!!!! We brought them home and we have loved them to pieces. The first six months was really hard, as they wake up in the middle of the night and we still were housetraining during that time. But, after that they became a part of the family. We crate trained them. They love to sleep in their crates. When we go somewhere they stay in their crates and do not roam around the house. When we go on family vacations, they come too!! One draw back is that it is like having a little baby again, you always have to think about what you are going to do with the puppies when you go somewhere. That was what was holding me back from saying "yes" in the first place. But, we have figured it out as we went along. Had my husband and I been by ourselves and the kids had already left home, we would have never had dogs!! But, we really felt our kids needed this experience, so we did it. By the way, we still have to remind our kids to feed, water, bathe, walk, etc.

SEWING
Learn to sew Videos
www.learn2sewvideo.com
-Very useful sewing fundamentals on DVD

Modest dressing
-Type this into your search engine and see the companies out there that believe in dressing modest! I was so impressed!

www.sewing.about.com
-Sewing patterns
-Used sewing machines
-Quilting

www.SewMoreForU.com
-Sewing Tips
-Patterns
-Pattern software

The Sophisticated Stitcher
www.thesophisticatedstitcher.com
-Needle craft of all kinds

60

The Big GIANT Decision...Homeschool!   By Penni Renee Pierce

You Can Make It
www.youcanmakeit.com
-"We teach a skill...not just a project."
-Instruction videos
-Learn to sew
-Learn to alter

SPECIAL NEEDS BOOKS & SITES with Learning Disability Resources

I am not afraid of storms, for I am learning how to sail my ship.

-Louisa May Alcott

www.audiblox2000.com
-Homeschooling resources for many learning disabilities

www.autism.com
-Resources

Best Homeschooling
www.besthomeschooling.org
-Homeschool site full of articles from other homeschoolers!

Early Communication Skills for Children with Down Syndrome: A Guide for Parents and Professionals
By Libby Kumin

Family Education
www.familyeducation.com
-Learning disabilities resource

Hands On Tasks and Ideas
www.hot-ideas.org

Home School Central
www.homeschoolcentral.com
-Homeschool resources
-Homeschool support groups
-Special Needs

61

The Big GIANT Decision...Homeschool!   By Penni Renee Pierce

Home School Views

www.homeschoolviews.com

-Advice from homeschooling families, including those who are homeschooling children with learning diabilities

Life Skills Activities for Special Children by Darlene Mannix

National Home Education Network

www.nhen.org

-Homeschool support

-Networking

-Special needs

-Gifted

Phillip Roy Inc.

www.philliproy.com

-See Special Education section on their site

62

The Big GIANT Decision...Homeschool!   By Penni Renee Pierce

MAGAZINES
Homeschool & Activity Magazines

About
www.homeschooling.about.com
-This site lists homeschool magazines and other publications.
-Great resource site

Fun For Kidz Magazines
www.funforkidzmagazines.com
-Includes Science, Math, Reading, Writing, Art, History, Cooking, Crafts, Contest, Pen Pal Club & Much more
-Supports family values
Hopscotch Magazine-designed for elementary age girls with no teen material! Also, no advertising!
Boys Quest- designed to help boys love reading in their youth, elementary age boys
Fun For Kidz Magazine- designed for both boys and girls

Growing Without School
www.fun-books.com
www.holtgws.com
-This magazine is no longer published, however you can purchase back issues.
-The first 2 years of GWS Magazine are now published in a book entitled "Growing Without School: A Record of a Grassroots Movement"

Home Education Magazine
www.homeedmag.com

Homeschooling Today Magazine
www.homeschooltoday.com

Nature Friend Magazine
www.dogwoodridgeoutdoors.com
-Color photos of all kinds of animals
-Nature puzzles, art projects, science experiments, fun-to-read stories

Practical Homeschooling Magazine
www.home-school.com

The Teaching Home
www.teachinghome.com

MATH
Books, Curricula, Manipulatives

If your child is having difficulty with certain math principles, for example "percentages", you can get workbooks just about percentages from any teachers store. There are many black line master books which you can make copies from if you have more than one child. You will just have to make the initial investment of one book.

Developmental Mathematics by L. George Saad, Ph.D.
-This is workbook style.
-The children can work on their own.
-Some homeschoolers do this program and then go directly into *Saxon* 54.

Family Math by Jean Kerr Stenmark, Ruth Cossey and Virgina Thompson.
-A great resource book with all kinds of games.
-You will see math in a whole new light.
-This now comes in two different books. One is for younger children ages 5-12 and then another book is for children ages 10-14.

Larson Learning Inc.
www.meridiancg.com
-Math products, K – 12th grade
-Larson's Elementary Math Activities are real-life math activities

Making Math Meaningful by David Quine
-This is a math curriculum.
- www.CornerstoneCurriculum.com
  214-235-5149

Math-It & Advanced Math-It
-Math-It starts at age five up through 6th grade and Advanced Math-It will continue on after that.
-I love the drills in Math-It.
-Very unique
-Look in the Catalogs & Materials section of this book and most homeschooling companies will have it.

65

The Big GIANT Decision...Homeschool!   By Penni Renee Pierce

Miquon Math by Key Curriculum Press
-You can purchase this from **Love to Learn** (Listed in the Catalogs & Materials section of this book)
-It is a math lab program that you use with the Cuisenaire rods, plastic rods of all different colors and sizes. Grades 1-3

Moving With Math Learning System
www.movingwithmath.com
Math Teachers Press, Inc.
-This program involves fun manipulatives
-Pre-K thru 8th grade

Saxon Math by Stephen Hake and John Saxon
-All of our children are using this math series. It is repetitive. I'm very pleased with it. After about every five lessons, there is a test. The kids check their lessons and their tests. We talk about the problems they missed and then they can always go back and look within those five lessons to see where they goofed up or misunderstood. The kids are very self-reliant in math. They are learning that there are many ways to figure a problem and all math problems can be worked out. Math frustration has been reduced 100 times since we started homeschool.
-If there is a math principle that someone is not understanding, there are sometimes practice problems in the back of the book for that principle. Or, sometimes I will purchase a workbook for that principle. For example, if someone is having a hard time with fractions, I get a workbook about fractions and start at the basics and move up to see where they start to misunderstand. School Zone Publishing Company, www.schoolzone.com have these workbooks and you can get them at just about any bookstore or teacher store or even toy stores.

66

The Big GIANT Decision...Homeschool!   By Penni Renee Pierce

MATH MATERIALS & MANIPULATIVES

Cuisenaire Rods
-These plastic rods of all different colors and lengths are fun to play with, but also teach math in a tangible way.
-The set comes with lots of ideas on how to use the rods.
-They can also be used with the Miquon math series.

Fraction Bars
-These are flat, plastic bars divided into different fractions.
-They are all different colors. You can play the suggested games with them or make up your own.
-I bought them at a teacher's store.

Saxon Math Manipulatives
-These should be purchased with any K-3 Saxon math books.
-They are a little expensive, but you get everything you need in a box and I feel that anything tangible used in the early years of learning math will help the principles and ideas of math to stick.
-Can be purchased from **Love to Learn** or **Lifetime Books and Gifts**

Triangle Flashcards
-These are triangle shaped flashcards.
-They are great for learning addition, subtraction, multiplication and division.
-They are different from your regular flashcards.
-Purchased at a teachers store

EXTRA NOTE: Other math manipulatives and math games can be purchased from **Love to Learn, The Always Incomplete Resource Guide and Catalog, The Home School Source Book** and others; see **Catalogs and Materials** section. Also, as you search the internet, there are oodles of Math manipulative resources.   Some sites even have free interactive manipulatives that are outstanding.   One, in particular, was done by Utah State University.   I don't know if their site will stay up, but I was very impressed with it (for grades 3-5).
The address is nlvm.usu.edu/en/nav/vlibrary.html

MUSIC
How I never spent a penny on music lessons!

BAND
New Creation Music
www.newcreationmusic.com
-Rent to own any instrument
-Entry level to master models
-Instrument accessories

Standard of Excellence Series
-For all different instruments
-Most commonly used practice books

MUSIC INTERNET SITES
www.jwpepper.com
-Resource for music books
-Teachers resources
-Music games

www.musictreasures.com
-Music awards
-Music & dance T-shirts
-They will mail a free catalog.

www.omegasound.com
-Great tracks for any voice range
-Some ensemble pieces and complete shows

PIANO
(Amy is my sister-in-law. She gave me many of the suggestions in this section. She has taught piano, voice and acting.)

Alfred Adult Series
-Amy likes these better than the kid series by Alfred.

Classical Jazz
Classical Movie Scenes by Phillip Keveren Series
-Varied levels

68

The Big GIANT Decision...Homeschool! By Penni Renee Pierce

David Carr Glover Series
-Amy recommends this. She uses this when she teaches piano.

Easy Favorites by Minstrel Press
-Beginning – Intermediate

Five Finger Piano by Hal Leonard
-For the very, very beginner
-A series
-Solo or duet form

Fundamentals of Piano Theory by Neil A. Kjos Music Company
-Great theory books at all levels
-Teacher editions available with all the answers

Jean Martin
-Jean Martin is a piano arranger.
-Great arrangements at all different piano levels
-**Holiday Dreams** is the name of one of her books.
-Her materials are put out by Neil A. Kjos Music Company

John Thompson's Modern Course for the Piano
-The girls enjoyed the beginning and advanced books from this series.
-My sister-in-law says that she likes the new ones that have recently come out.

Rock Jazz Course (the one for adults) by Alfred
-Can be used if you have had one year of piano or more

Faber & Faber Piano Adventures
-Amy likes this, too!
-You can use as supplemental music.

Scales- Alfred's Scales, Chords and Arpeggios
-I think it is important for part of the piano practice to include practicing scales.
-You can get books that have only scales and teach correct fingering.

The SJH Pianist Curriculum by Helen Marlais
-Piano duets
-Comes with CD's

69

The Big GIANT Decision...Homeschool! By Penni Renee Pierce

Usborne
-This company makes all kinds of books.   They have produced some beginner piano books that we have used. Also, they have some beginner classical music books for piano that we use all the time.

The World's Great Classical Music Favorite Classical Themes by Hal Leonard
-Easy (one year of piano) – Intermediate piano solos

VOICE
(Amy is my sister-in-law. She has taught piano, voice and acting. She recommends these voice books.)

Basics of Singing by Jan Schmidt
-Text book for singers of all ages with cassettes or CD's

Broadway Full Dress Performance by Hal Leonard

Encores For Solo Singers by Alfred
-For intermediate and advanced singers

The First Book of Soprano Solos by Schirmer
-Available in all voice parts (S.A.T.B.)
-Distributed thru Hal Leonard

Folk Songs for Two by Alfred

The Kids Broadway Song Book by Hal Leonard
-Contains songs sung on Broadway by children

Popular Solos For Kids by Hal Leonard

The Singers Gilbert & Sullivan by Hal Leonard
-Men's and women's edition
-Jr. high - up

Solos For Kids by Hal Leonard
-Several versions including Solos for Kids Broadway, Solos for Kids Disney, etc.

70

The Big GIANT Decision...Homeschool!   By Penni Renee Pierce

Standard Vocal Literature by Hal Leonard
-Comes in the voice range needed
-Comes with diction lessons on CD

The Teen's Musical Theatre Collection
Young Men/Young Women Edition by Hal Leonard

36 Solos For Young Singers by Hal Leonard

EXTRA MUSIC NOTES: MUSIC FAMILY HISTORY
Music is a part of our lives. My great grandmother played the banjo and sang. My granny played guitar and sang. She and my grandfather were in yodeling contests. My two uncles have incredible singing voices. My mother is a professional singer, performer and audio engineer. My step-dad is a professional guitarist, performer and audio engineer as well. I was practically raised in a recording studio. My husband Mark is a musician and was actually majoring in music, until he realized he had to make a real living. Hee! So, the fact that our kids have turned out to be very good musicians was not a huge surprise. Music is a very fun part of our lives.   Briana, Kyla and Tahnee have recently learned to harmonize some of the old Andrew Sisters songs. They practiced everyday for several months and then recorded in a studio. It was a great deal of work, not to mention lots of fun for them.

EXTRA NOTES: HOW I TAUGHT MY DAUGHTERS TO PLAY THE PIANO
I do not play the piano. I play the flute. But, I have taught all my daughters to play the piano and they are amazing. We have never spent a penny on piano lessons!!!! I taught them basic theory. You know, a quarter note equals one count, etc. We did purchase beginner piano books and went from there. The secret was making piano practice time a part of our school day and then I would give a lesson or two every now and again. They had to practice 30 - 60 minutes per day depending on the kid. Rachel and Briana did wonderfully with this idea. Tahnee and Kyla had to be bribed. First of all, there was no choice about practicing. They had to do it every school day. I did give our son a choice between piano or another instrument, though. He chose saxophone. That lasted a couple of months and then he chose the guitar and he plays fantastically on the guitar. I had to tell Tahnee that if she practiced for an entire

71

The Big GIANT Decision...Homeschool!   By Penni Renee Pierce

month she would get to go to her favorite store and pick something out. It seemed to work for her. But, I sure do get flack about it now, even from Tahnee. She says, "Mom, I was being a brat. You spoiled me." Of course, I didn't care at the time, I only know that it worked. Oh yes, you know all of those times when you are giving your children a discourse about, "when you were little"? Well, I gave one of those stories once to Tahnee about my own experience taking piano lessons. I told her that when I was seven years old I quit piano because I didn't want to practice and how badly I have felt since then, because I have not learned to play the piano even to this day. I had actually forgotten about telling her that story, when one day she said that that story is the reason why she really started practicing more and stuck with it!!!! Can you believe it? She actually listened to me and felt my pain!! So, don't discount your discourses! Someone could actually be listening. The girls have done wonderfully on the piano and have played at church and accompanied singers and musicians.

OUR CHILDREN'S BOOK REVIEW
Mark, Rachel, Tahnee, Briana, & Kyla

Mark, 13 years old
The Hobbit by J.R.R. Tolkien
-It is the best fantasy book I have read.
-It makes you want to read more.
Black Cauldron series by Lloyd Alexander
-Good
The Chronicles of Narnia by C.S. Lewis
-Good
Genghis Khan and the Mongol Horde by Harold Lamb (Landmark Book)
-I liked the part when Genghis Khan's army attempted to take over half the world!

Rachel, 12 years old
Little House on the Prairie series by Laura Ingalls Wilder
-I have read 5 of them and I am on the 6th one. They are wonderful books about Laura's life. I love them!
The American Girls Collection by different authors
-I've read *Meet Addy*
              Meet Samantha
-I recommend these books.
-They tell about young girls in their different historical times.
Beauty
A Dog Called Kitty
Danger on Panther Peak
Danger in Quicksand Swamp
Trapped in Death Cave
All of these by Bill Wallace
-These are the books that made me excited about reading!!
-The way they are written makes you want to read on and on!
The Canada Geese Quilt by Natalie Kisey Warnock
-I liked this.

Tahnee, 10 years old
Little House on the Prairie series by Laura Ingalls Wilder
-These books are about her life and they are really, really good!
Indian in the Cupboard by Lynne Reid Banks
-This was a neat book!

-It was exciting to think that the toys could come to life!
Pee Wee Scout series by Judy Delten
-These are easy to read.
-You can read the whole series pretty quick.
-I like how they work out their problems to earn their badges.
Charlotte's Web by E.B. White
-I like the rat, he's funny!

Everyone's Favorite Read-Alouds

Heidi by Johanna Spyri
Johnny Tremain by Esther Forbes
Daniel Boone by Augusta Stevenson (From the Childhood of Famous Americans series)
The Blackfoot by Elizabeth Hahn
If You Lived in Colonial Times by Ann McGovern
Early Health and Medicine by Bobbie Valman
Helen Keller by Katharine E. Wilkie (From the Childhood of Famous Americans series)
The Secret Garden by Frances Hodgson Burnett

Briana's and Kyla's Book List of Favorites

(We especially enjoyed all of these, but if there is a star beside the title, we really, really liked it and it could possibly be worth purchasing)
(Briana and Kyla age 41/2 & 3)
Alphabet City by Stephen T. Johnson
One Hundred Hungry Ants by Elinor J. Pinczes
Pretend You're A Cat by Jean Marzollo
Growing Colors by Bruce McMillan
Corduroy by Don Freeman
Yertle the Turtle & Other Stories by Dr. Seuss
Chipmunk Song by Joanne Ryder
Peter's Pockets by Eve Rice
Olly's Pollywogs by Anne & Harlow Rockwell
Apples to Zippers (An Alphabet Book) by Patricia Ruben
The Way Home by Judith Benet Richardson
Piggy Washes Up by Carol Thompson
Over On the Farm by Christopher Gunson

(Briana and Kyla ages 5 & 4)
Toolchest - A primer of Woodcraft by Jan Adkins
Mouseskin's ABC by Edna Miller

74

The Big GIANT Decision...Homeschool!   By Penni Renee Pierce

The Giant Nursery Book of Things That Work by George J. Zaffo
Tool Book by Gail Gibbons

(Briana and Kyla ages 6 & 41/2)
Miss Rumphius by Barbara Cooney
The Mare On The Hill by Thomas Locker
Caterpillar Caterpillar by Vivian French
You Be Good & I'll Be Night by Eve Merriam
Eggbert (The Slightly Cracked Egg) by Tom Ross
Mud Pies & Other Recipes by Marjorie Winslow
Lucy Comes to Stay by Rosemary Wells
The Long, Long Letter by Elizabeth Spurr
All About Alfie by Shirley Hughes
Hold My Hand by Charlotte Zolotow
Arthur's Computer Disaster by Marc Brown
Goodnight Andrew, Goodnight Craig by Marjorie Sharmat
Gladys Told Me To Meet Her Here by Marjorie Sharmat
The Big Fat Enormous Lie by Marjorie Sharmat
The Summer Sands by Sherry Garland
Stories For Under Five-Year-Olds edited by Sara & Stephen Corrin
There are also *Stories For Five-Year-Olds*
               Stories For Six-Year-Olds
               Stories For Seven-Year-Olds
When I Was Young In The Mountain by Cynthia Rylant
Toddlerobics by Zita Newcome (Some may consider this a toddler book, but my 5 & 6 year olds loved the cute drawings of babies doing aerobic exercises!)
The Relatives Came by Cynthia Rylant

(Briana and Kyla ages 7 & 6)
The Sign On Rosie's Door by Maurice Sendak
Very Far Away by Maurice Sendak
When Jessie Came Across The Sea by Amy Hest & Illustrated by P.J. Lynch (true story)
Imagine You Are A Tiger by Karen Wallace & Peter Melnyczuk
Henry And Mudge by Cynthia Rylant
If You Give A Pig A Pancake by Laura Numeroff
Two Bad Ants by Chris Van Allsburg
A Colt Named Mischief by Sandy Rabinowitz
Poppleton by Cynthia Rylant

75

The Big GIANT Decision...Homeschool!   By Penni Renee Pierce

Mr. Putter & Tabby Pick The Pears by Cynthia Rylant
Mr. Putter & Tabby Toot The Horn by Cynthia Rylant
The Grannyman by Judith Byron Schachner
Bonesy & Isabel by Michael J. Rosen

Other Favorites
All of a Kind Family (series) by Sidney Taylor
-About a sweet Jewish family
The Hiding Place by Corrie ten Boom
-Takes place during WW II
-A Dutch family hides Jews in their home.

EXTRA NOTE: Below Briana and Kyla give a book review at the ages of 12 and 14.

Briana's Book Review (age 14)
Children of the Promise Series by Dean Hughes
It's written in the 40's era, my favorite time period. These books helped me to learn more about World War II. It is a historical fiction. It has several love stories going on, however they are very sweet and wholesome love stories! There are five books in the series. They are about 400 to 500 pages. I read all of them and I was very interested the whole time! Some really sad things happen in war torn Germany when the Nazi's took over. So, I would recommend teenagers to adult age reading.

The Rise and Fall of Adolph Hitler by William Shirer
This book helped me to understand more about how Hitler became involved in politics and worked his way up and gradually became corrupt and evil. Something I do not understand is how he ever got away with the things he did!!!!

Kyla's Book Review (age 12)
Johnny Tremain by Esther Forbes
This book was about a boy who was an apprentice to a silversmith during the 1700's. At the time, England is in charge of the thirteen colonies. America is about to have the Revolutionary War. I liked the friendship between Cilla and Johnny. Isannah was a little brat!

76

The Big GIANT Decision…Homeschool! By Penni Renee Pierce

Secret Garden by Frances Hodgson Burnett

This was a magical book! The little girl was very stubborn, but soon changes. I like the way she finds the garden. We also watched the movie after we had read the book. The book has more details and the movie changes the story in some places making it not at all like the book.

77

The Big GIANT Decision...Homeschool!   By Penni Renee Pierce

OUT-OF-PRINT BOOKS TO CHERISH
List Of Books

Thanks to my friend, Christie Atkinson, listed below are books worth the search!

A Child's History of the World
A Child's History of Art
A Child's Geography of the World
all of these by V. M. Hillyer

America Is Born - A History for Peter
by Gerald W. Johnson

American Heritage Series
published by American Heritage Publishing Company
-I love these because of the real photos, maps and beautiful paintings.

Landmark Books (all hardbacks are out-of-print)
-American history and world history

Myths and Enchantment Tales
by Margaret Evans Price

Michael O'Halloran
The Keeper of the Bees
by Gene Stratton-Porter

Twin Series
The American Twins of the Revolution
The Dutch Twins
by Lucy Fitch Perkins

Young Masters of Music
by Mary Newlin Roberts

REFERENCE BOOKS
List Of Books Worth Purchasing

I recommend picking up your reference books at discount book stores.

Almanacs
Atlas'
Do-It-Yourself Books
-We have gardening books, carpentry books, car repair books, decorating books, sewing books, cookbooks, remodeling books, game and party books, etc.

-*EXTRA NOTE: Since writing the first edition, we have spent the last five years restoring a 100 year old home and doing all of the work ourselves. We have acquired many "Do-It-Yourself" books since then on: roofing, chimneys, electrical wiring, plumbing, leveling and restoring floors, etc.*

Encyclopedias
-We use these just about every day! And they are 20 years old!
The Encyclopedia of Country Living by Carla Emery
-This book teaches you everything you need to know about living in the country and I mean everything! You can purchase it from **Love to Learn** (see Catalog section)
First Aid Books
Guinness Books
Herb Books
Hobby Books
-Coin collecting, stamp collecting, old dolls, trains, etc.
Medical Books
Nutrition Books
Scouting Books
-These books have a lot of useful information and lesson ideas!
Thesaurus
Webster's Dictionary
-We have some small paperback ones
-But, the one that is most useful is our large, awkward one that is called "The Living Webster Encyclopedic Dictionary of the English Language"

All men by nature desire knowledge.
-Aristotle

The Big GIANT Decision...Homeschool! By Penni Renee Pierce

79

SCHOLARSHIPS
A HOMESCHOOL GRADUATE'S ADVICE ON SEEKING SCHOLARSHIPS

Our daughter, Tahnee graduated from homeschool several years ago. She says:

1) Start early in your search for scholarships.
2) Organize a hard copy file to keep "letters of recommendation" from teachers or employers, several copies of college transcripts (some scholarships require a copy to be sent with your application), several copies of high school transcripts, keep an updated list of your community volunteer work, your extracurricular activities, sports participation, awards, etc.
3) Watch and keep track of scholarship deadline dates and work on the scholarships that need to be turned in first. You may want to keep an organized file in date order.
4) DO NOT apply for scholarship adds that say, for example, "$10,000.00 scholarship, FAST & EASY, all you need do is enter your name and email address!" Thousands of people are applying for these and then *your* email address is used to send you junk mail.
5) Look at applying for scholarships as homework. You have to do it in order to get one and *it is* work!
6) Look for the scholarships that require a lot of work on your part, i.e. essays, personal accomplishments, etc.
7) GOOD LUCK!

Tahnee recommends this site for scholarship searching. www.scholarshipexperts.com

Whatever you are, be a good one.
-Abraham Lincoln

80

The Big GIANT Decision...Homeschool! By Penni Renee Pierce

SCHOOLS
Online, Distance Learning, Correspondence

SCHOOL CHOICE

You may be considering some kind of alternative education. Taking your child out of public school may seem scary and overwhelming. Here is a way that may help you gain confidence and will help prove that learning can really occur at home. Correspondence schooling has become popular. It takes the pressure off of *you*. Some schools take care of paperwork. But, in most cases you will still be under a structure created by a school. You may love it, you may dislike it. You may decide to do this for the first year and then do your own thing the next. It might be a good idea to get information from all of these schools before deciding. I've heard nice things about all of them. Also, I have listed below a few colleges too!

ACCREDITATION

Did you know that accreditation is done on a voluntary basis? You probably did, but I just researched this recently and found out. Accreditation organizations are private organizations. The United States Department of Education will approve organizations if they meet with certain criteria, however. But, the organizations do not have to be approved by the USDE. Some schools want this USDE "stamp of approval". Even though accreditation is on a voluntary basis only, some colleges and universities will not accept a transcript from an incoming student unless it is from an accredited school. So, keep that in mind as you are homeschooling through high school. There are regional organizations, national organizations and some specialty school accreditation organizations. If you visit www.chea.org, you will be able to view an updated list of recognized accreditation organizations. You will want to check to make sure that the school you have chosen is accredited by a legitimate organization. In the state of Texas, a homeschool is considered a private school and I have not had a problem, as of yet, sending my kids to community college. Our Private School Homeschool Transcript has been acceptable. However, I am keeping on top of this in case the rules change, because we could waste a great deal of time. You may want to learn what it means for a school to be "accredited".

Here are some more sites that will shed some light on accreditation: **The Meaning and Value of Accreditation,** www.neasc.org; **The National Charter School Clearing House,** www.ncsc.info; **Accredited Schools Information,** www.uceadirectory.org; **Distance Learning Accreditation,** www.elearners.com.

The Big GIANT Decision...Homeschool!   By Penni Renee Pierce

81

I have never let my schooling interfere with my education.
-Mark Twain

ABC- Homeschool
www.abc-homeschool.com
-Includes a list of accredited homeschools
-Lots of information!

Alger Learning Center & Independence High School
1-800-595-2630
www.independent-learning.com
-Private school
-K thru 12
-Alger supports the unschooling idea and will help you design a course of study to fit your child's interests and background.
-Nationally accredited

Bob Jones University
864-242-5100
www.bju.edu
BJU HomeSat (Satellite School)
call 1-800-739-8199 for a video demo
-You can buy their curricula separately or you can enroll in their school.
-If you enroll for grades 9-12, you can receive a diploma when complete.

Calvert School
1-888-487-4652
www.calvertschool.org
-PreK – 8th grade

Christian Liberty Academy
847-259-4444
www.homeschools.org
-K – 12th grade

82

The Big GIANT Decision...Homeschool!   By Penni Renee Pierce

The College Board
www.collegeboard.org
-A college resource site

CurriculumFair.com
www.CurriculumFair.com
-Listings of online or distance learning schools, colleges.
-Continuing education, degrees

ED Anywhere
1-877-433-0805
www.edanywhere.com
-A resource site
-Certified teaching assistance
-Assessment testing
-Transcripts for homeschoolers

George Wythe College
435-586-6570
www.gwc.edu
-Their mission: *To build men and women of virtue, wisdom, diplomacy and courage who inspire greatness in others and move the cause of liberty.*

K12 Online School
www.k12.com
-Provides K – 12th grade curricula
-Placement testing
-This looks like a good site if you want the curriculum already chosen for you.

Laurel Springs School
1-800-377-5890
www.laurelsprings.com
-Accredited Private School, K-12

83

The Big GIANT Decision...Homeschool! By Penni Renee Pierce

Oak Meadow
802-251-7250
www.oakmeadow.com
-K-12
-accredited

Oral Roberts University
1-800-678-8876
www.oru.edu
-Homeschool College Preparatory Program

Pearblossom Private School
1-800-309-3569
www.pearblossomschool.com
-Quality Educational Programs
-K thru 12
-Nationally accredited
-Equestrian division

Penn Foster High School
www.penfoster.edu
-Nationally and regionally accredited
-High school diploma

SAT/ACT, Online Guide
www.testprep.com
-Practice SAT & ACT
-Scholarship information

School of Tomorrow
1-800-925-7777 Orders
972-315-1776
www.schooloftomorrow.com
-Homeschool materials thru Lighthouse Christian Academy (1-866-746-6534)
-Accredited

84

The Big GIANT Decision…Homeschool!   By Penni Renee Pierce

The Sycamore Tree
Center for Home Education
1-800-779-6750
www.sycamoretree.com
-Complete homeschool program
-Pre-K thru 12th grade
-Accredited

85

The Big GIANT Decision...Homeschool! By Penni Renee Pierce

SCIENCE
Projects, Experiments, Health, etc.

Be careful about reading health books. You may die of a misprint.
-Mark Twain

All About books (For example: *All About Whales, All About the Stars,* etc.)
We collect these also. I've had several people say their children enjoy these. Marguerite Henry wrote the *All About Horses* book. Some are outdated, such as *All About Atomic Energy.* But, my friend's 15-year-old son read this book and enjoyed reading what was written about atomic energy 20 or more years ago. Of course, up-to-date stuff is essential when it comes to science. Also, if I find a nice book about penguins or whales or birds I will get it, especially if it has real pictures. Science and Nature books are just fun to have on hand for rainy day activities!

Answers About Rocks and Minerals by Frederick Smithline
-Library book
-Includes lots of questions to get the kids thinking

Backyard Scientist by Jane Hoffman
-This is a series for all different ages.
-Easy to use
-Gives many questions to ask the kids after they have done their observation

Blood and Guts by Linda Allison
-Has lots of different experiments to do to learn about the human body
-Kids will love this one

Celebrate the Feasts of the Old Testament in Your Own
Home or Church by Martha Zimmerman
-I guess you're wondering why I have this book listed with the science books.
-Refer to my Science Notes in the **Why We Did It! How You Can Do it!** section to see why.

Chemically Active by Vicki Cobb
-Makes the experimenter think
-Asks the student many questions

86

The Big GIANT Decision...Homeschool!   By Penni Renee Pierce

Dinosaurs For Every Kid, Janice VanCleave's

by Janice Van Cleave
"Easy Activities That Make Learning Science Fun"
-I used this with Briana and Kyla at age 5 and 6, but I was only able to use a couple of things for their level.
-However, this would be great to use at about age 10 - up.
-Janice Van Cleave has written many books about different science topics for children of all ages.

The Golden Nature Guides or The Golden Guides

-These are those small books that are field guides.
-We collect these.
-They have come in handy when one of the kids has a question about a rock, shell, insect or bird.
-You probably have some of your own.
-I find them at book sales all the time.

Home Science Tools

www.homesciencetools.com
-I love science. This site will make you want to have science class all the time.
-Science gear!!
-Microscopes
-Earth science, biology, forensic
-Science curriculum

How Do Our Eyes See

by Carol Ballard
From series called: *How Your Body Works*
-Very good
-Includes information about Braille, optometrists, parts of the eye and color blindness

How To Be An Inventor

by Murray Suid
-The steps of an inventor
-How to get a patent

How To Teach Nutrition To Kids by Connie Liakos Evers, MS, RD

-Ages 6 - 10, but can be adapted for older children
-Great ideas and activities

-Even teaches about reading labels on food packages
-Integrates Social Studies, Language Arts, Math, Science, Art & P.E.
-I really like this book!

Human Anatomy Coloring Book by Margaret Matt
text by Joe Ziemian (A Dover Coloring Book)
-Clear illustrations and good text
-You may want to purchase some good quality colored pencils with lots of color choices.
-This book will end up being a great reference book.

The Human Body* by Ruth Dowling Bruun, M.D. and Bertel Bruun, M.D.
-Excellent illustrations

Kids Gardening
by Kevin Raftery and Kim Gilbert Raftery
-Great for kids and adults!
-Tells many things about gardening
-Great illustrations
-Comes with seeds and small spade

Lenses! Take A Closer Look
by Siegfried Aust
From series called: *Fun With Technology*
-I love this book.
-Includes information about the history of lenses, microscopes and telescopes

Opt
by Arline & Joseph Baum
-A book of optical illusions
-Great fun while studing the eyeball and sight

Real Science-4-Kids
Gravitas Publications
www.gravitaspublications.com
-Real science introduces Chemistry, Biology and Physics from 1st grade and up!
-Curriculum K – 9th grade

88

The Big GIANT Decision...Homeschool!   By Penni Renee Pierce

Simple Science Experiments with Everyday Materials
by Muriel Mandell
-Fun book and includes historical tidbits like, the history of paper

The Usborne Book of Science, An introduction to Biology, Physics and Chemistry
-Great resource book

*Books recommended by homeschooling friends.

EXTRA NOTE: Some science books will refer to evolution. I do not agree with evolution, but I skip over it or sometimes we discuss it so the kids know what is right. Reference to evolution does not make the whole book un-usable, the other material in the book may be excellent. If your child is interested in science, it would be a good idea for him to know other science theories, i.e. evolution. You cannot be knowledgeable in science unless you know what *other* scientists believe.

89

The Big GIANT Decision...Homeschool! By Penni Renee Pierce

SUPPORT GROUPS
The Author's Thoughts & Links To Find Them All!

If you have knowledge, let others light their candles with it.
—Sir Winston Churchill

What Are Your Homeschool Needs?

Support groups come in all different sizes and shapes. They may be very large and organized. They may be very small and casual. Some Homeschool Support Groups may organize many activities outside the home, which may not be the way you want to do things. On the other hand, the support from other parents who are homeschooling their children and the interaction with other children may be just what you want. You will have to be the judge of how much time will be spent with a support group outside the home.

Where Are The Support Groups Located?

There are many ways to get lists of support groups. Many of the homeschooling magazines will have support groups listed in the back by state or the magazine web sites have links to support groups. I was going to include a list of support groups by state here, but they change so often that the information might not remain up-to-date. The best way, as of yet, is to go to the Homeschool Legal Defense Association web site and look up support groups for your state (www.hslda.org). They list the state organizations and then you can click your county and get even more localized support. This is an excellent site for all other homeschooling information, too. Also, many YMCA's have classes and support for homeschoolers.

Support Group Activities

One year I directed a Homeschool Choir. We had about twenty children and we performed a couple of times for parents and relatives. It was so much fun. The kids were great singers and we learned a lot. It was also exciting for the kids to get together once a week for choir and the moms had fun too! So, choir could be a way to start a support group. Some parents help and support each other by trading teaching. For example, one parent teaches history and another teaches language arts and they go to each other's homes. Sometimes parents will teach science in the summer to a group of homeschool kids. One year Briana and Kyla took an Earth Science class at the Heard Museum here in Texas. They had access to the museum grounds and classrooms. One of the staff members taught the class and they had the opportunity to use microscopes.

GETTING STARTED CHECK LIST
Easy Check List To Start Homeschooling Now!

_____Decide if homeschooling is *right* for your family.

_____Have the support of your spouse.

_____Find out your state laws for homeschooling (See **The Law** section or visit www.hslda.org)

_____Locate a support group in your state (www.hslda.org)

_____Know the subjects required by law

_____Decide any subjects you would like to add to the required subjects

_____Read and find out the books or curricula that are available for your subjects (Familiarize yourself with the **Catalogs and Materials** section of this book)

_____Purchase only the *required* subject books first (This will help minimize your initial costs)

_____Write down your goals of what you plan to achieve with each child (short-term and long-term)

_____Decide how to organize your homeschooling day and have a schedule (See **Our Daily Schedule.**)

_____Get the *Always Incomplete Resource Guide and Catalog* by Bob and Tina Farewell (online and CD only) www.lifetimebooksandgifts.com

_____Call 1-877-375-4680 and order Donn Reed's book *The Home School Source Book* or visit www.brookfarmbooks.com

_____Read homeschool success books, such as *Homeschooling for Excellence* by David and Micki Colfax.
(See **How-To, Self-Help & Resource Books** section)

_____Make a list of school materials you will need and start gathering things together, such as glue, scissors, tape, stapler, colored paper, pens, pencils, etc.

_____Get a computer. Save for it. Get a computer!

_____If you have completed this check list, you are ready to begin homeschooling your children!!

EXTRA NOTE: The **Getting Started Check List,** is basically a commitment from you to go forward in educating yourself and your family about homeschool. Then you can begin to get organized and gather the things that you need. Beware of overspending when choosing curricula. There will be so many fun, exciting things to do with your children, you may want them all!! But, if you will just stick to what is required as you are learning to homeschool, then as you go along you will be able to add extra things.

92

The Big GIANT Decision...Homeschool!   By Penni Renee Pierce

WHY WE DID IT!
HOW YOU CAN DO IT!
Detailed Notes Of Our Homeschool Experience

(Many of the notes were written when we first began homeschool and as I compiled the Third Edition of The Big Giant Decision, we have been homeschooling now for 13 years, so I have added Extra Notes to further explain our experiences. Of course, the sections added about Homeschool Graduates are from our experience now that we have three graduates of our own!)

The Big GIANT Decision...Homeschool! By Penni Renee Pierce

93

Chapter 1
FREE TO LEARN
An article about school frustration
-by Penni Renee Pierce

For several years we had three of our children coming home from school, frustrated, tired and not happy. They were laden with assignment after assignment and standardized test after standardized test! Their teachers were under a tremendous amount of stress. Regulations and pressure from the school districts were trickling down into the classrooms. Learning was no longer fun.

The feeling in the classroom was, "Hurry up and learn this principle, because we need to complete this book by the end of the year." A child being able to spend extra time on something, they really enjoy, was unheard of. Our children's natural desire to learn was being suffocated by the structure and endless material that MUST be covered in a school year.

We, as parents, have little control over this pressure. But, we have an alternative. It's a challenging alternative. It takes a lot of thought, organization and sacrifice. It may not be for all people, but it is definitely worth considering. Homeschooling your children is a challenge. But anything worthwhile has far reaching rewards. Seeing a child change, from despising history and reading to absolutely loving it, is truly a reward.

There are many parents and children who would like to, but cannot do homeschool at this time for one reason or another. I hope the children will be able to hang in there. Most of them will be fine, but many will not.

As for the child that makes it through the public school system and "does fine"; let's just suppose for a moment that this child loved animals and it was their dream to be a forest ranger or veterinarian. Just imagine if this child had been able to learn math, history, reading, etc. through this love of animals; what kind of an impact could this have? What kind of passion for learning could be rekindled? Could this child's feelings have been changed from "learning being a chore" to " learning being a joy"?

It's interesting to see children that have freedom to learn. They start to have ambition. They start to feel a desire to know more. They are interested in many things. They are not afraid to try new things. They have an opinion. They re-gain an appetite for learning because they're given the chance and <u>time</u> to think about things, research them, write about and discuss them. Also, their perception of time changes. They don't watch the clock to see if homeschool is over. They know and realize that learning continues throughout all the waking hours. They don't feel the pressure to "hurry up" with a science procedure in which they are interested. They're free. And they're FREE TO LEARN.

I do not know the answers for our public schools. However, I do ask myself, "Is "keeping up with the Jones" or another school district or whomever we're trying to keep up with, worth the mental fatigue of a third grader?

The burden is an unspoken, unwritten competition between school districts. The children are translating it as, "learning is not fun". Many school children will endure the burden created by the school system. Some will barely drag it across the stage on graduation day and a lot of children will let go and quit! They may graduate, but mentally they do not care.

As for those parents who are curious about homeschool and for those who "sort-of", "kind-of", "maybe-might" want to homeschool their children, this book will help!

I'm thankful to be able to write this book. It is not a book written to oppose public schooling. There are many talented and dedicated teachers, who are sincerely trying to teach. However, I hope the things written here will help to erase the often misunderstood idea of homeschooling and guide the reader to the conclusion that homeschooling is a real and feasible educational alternative. It is possible for a child to be very excited about learning. Here is our story.

EXTRA NOTE: Twelve years later, after writing "Free To Learn", I found this quote by Albert Einstein that expresses this curiosity and desire to learn that exists in us all.

It is, in fact, nothing short of a miracle that the modern methods of instruction have not yet entirely strangled the holy curiosity of inquiry; for this delicate little plant, aside from stimulation, stands mainly in need of freedom; without this it goes to wrack and ruin without fail. It is a very grave mistake to think that the enjoyment of seeing and searching can be promoted by means of coercion and a sense of duty. To the contrary, I believe that it would be possible to rob even a healthy beast of prey of its voraciousness, if it were possible, with the aid of a whip, to force the beast to devour continuously, even when not hungry, especially if the food, handed out under such coercion, were to be selected accordingly.

—Albert Einstein

The Big GIANT Decision...Homeschool! By Penni Renee Pierce

95

Chapter 2
OUR STORY
How we began 14 years ago...

Homeschool changed our lives so much. Here's why we decided to homeschool, what we have accomplished and even problems we have encountered.

We have five children, ages 13, 12, 10, 3 and 2. When we started homeschool they were 12, 11, 9, 2 and 1. Our three oldest have attended public school since kindergarten. They did very well academically. However, there were some things with which we were not pleased.

No Fun

When our two oldest reached second grade, school was no longer fun. In their first couple of years they would run out of school with happy faces and painted pictures blowing in the wind. But in second grade, at the end of the day, they came to the car looking like they had been at a hard day's work.

"Top Notch"

Our children attended in a school district considered to be "top notch". The teachers seemed to be under a great deal of pressure that came from the school district. In turn, the children were being taught by stressed-out teachers. When our second child was in third grade, we were at our wits end. We were tired of the stress imposed upon our children. I was tired of them bringing home assignments, which had been part of my 10th grade curriculum.

Public School Text Choices

I went to the third grade teacher, whom I admired, trying to find out how to complain about the curricula in a tactful way. In particular, I did not approve of the social studies and math books. She told me that she was on the committee that helped choose these books. She informed me that many hours had been spent on these choices. I could tell that my opinion was not going to matter much. The entire situation made me feel that my job was to be Rachel's mother (which, by the way, is a total privilege and joy!), and the decisions regarding textbooks needed to be made by people with much higher understanding and teaching degrees. I realize the teachers and administrators either do not have time to listen to or are not inclined to listen to parent's opinions on text choices. Many parents do not want the responsibility of choosing these.

96

The Big GIANT Decision...Homeschool!   By Penni Renee Pierce

Something's Missing?

Despite this, we tried to stay involved. We attended P.T.A., an organization, which I feel, is sincerely trying to bridge the gap between the parents and teachers. But, I knew I wasn't involved in my child's education even if I did sew lion costumes for the school production; baked cookies for the bake sale; went from business to business asking for donations for the school carnival; ordered and purchased recess equipment. Don't get me wrong, these are worthwhile activities. There was just something missing between the families and the school system. There was something missing in my children's faces and attitudes about learning. The BIG question was: HOW were WE helping with our children's education?

Learning + Reading = Nightmare!

Here's how I saw the whole picture. Our 11-year-old hated to read. So, when her social studies test would come up, I would read one page and she would read the other. We would discuss it and literally cram for her tests. She hated history. I would ask her what she was studying this week and she would say, "I don't really know. Some war, I think!" I felt bad. She was not enjoying learning. Reading was a chore for her, even though she was an excellent reader and an "A" and "B" student. Book reports were a nightmare.

Scream, Stomp and Pull Your Hair Out!

I would help my son anguish through reports about which he cared nothing. I tried to make him care, which we all know is an impossible task. My husband and I would try to make it interesting. In math, we would help him with principles that weren't clear. Our son would say that his teacher had explained it differently, so his mother and father must be wrong. It was so hard sometimes, I wanted to scream!! I didn't feel we had an alternative. I felt the answer to my BIG question (HOW were WE helping with our children's education?) was that we were evidently suppose to teach them at night after they had spent a seven hour day at school. We were cramming for tests with them. We were trying to help them enjoy learning. But, what can you do with a child after he has spent seven hours in a classroom? He is saturated and burned out!!

Stolen Family Time

The teachers had spent seven hours with them and then had given them assignments here and there with all different guidelines and due dates and had taken away any family time we might have had together. Our time with our children was frustrating. How were we helping with their education? We were teaching them at home after school, that's how! I felt this was so unfair to our family.

97

The Big GIANT Decision...Homeschool! By Penni Renee Pierce

Our Kids Are Tough, They Can Handle It!

However, all I knew I could do was to help them get through it. Somehow, just help them make it through, like I had to do when I was in public school and everyone else has to do, also. There were no different roads to take. "Our kids are tough, they can handle it!" Besides, there was no way I could change the school district's pressure on the teachers and the pressure the children feel from the teachers.

Boo! Hiss! Standardized Tests! Boo! Hiss!

I also did not feel good about the way standardized tests were handled. The kids were being drilled and drilled for these tests, so that the school districts could hold or raise their rank. They drilled the children for a week or more, then on test day the children were told that the test was "no big deal" and to "just do your best" and "take your time". I felt two messages were being sent: 1) This test is important enough to take a whole week to drill and 2) This test is "no big deal". Which is it? Kids don't know <u>what</u> to think about these tests; neither do parents!

Pretend you are a new teacher.
You need to test the students in math and reading
to know their level of understanding.
Would you have them study for this test?

I was so furious when our children would come home with worksheets to study for a "standardized test", plus regular homework! Somewhere, someone has lost the point of these tests. The results have become meaningless, as far as I'm concerned. If your school district rates high in the nation, I would check to see how much emphasis is put on standardized testing. How much of your child's "learning time" is being used to teach test answers?

Homeschool? Not Me, Never!

At this point, my thoughts on homeschool were that I knew people that homeschooled, but I would never do it! I thought it was eccentric and the children would suffer socially and, frankly, I didn't want to do it or even think I could. I didn't know the presidents of Yale and Princeton were homeschooled!!

"Our School District Is Fine!"

During this time, also, we were in the process of finding a home to buy. The anguish we felt was, "What about the schools?!!" We knew that once we decided to buy, we were stuck with that school district. It was so scary. We visited schools. I called schools. I

98

The Big GIANT Decision...Homeschool!   By Penni Renee Pierce

spoke to parents and PTA presidents. Everyone said their school districts were fine. Of course, no one wants to think they're sending their children to a "less than perfect" environment. So, I knew this input was not the whole picture. I prayed. We both prayed. I had always asked Heavenly Father to help me make good decisions. I prayed for this all the time. I knew that we would be directed in our lives, but I also knew Heavenly Father gave me a brain to make decisions. In this case, our lives were being directed and there was going to be a major change.

Homeschool? Not Unless Angels Came And Told Me To Do It!

My special friend, Christie Atkinson, has homeschooled four of her five children (one is in college). I admire her for homeschooling and being very successful for three years. One day I called her to check on her daughter, who had been absent from my Sunday School class. I asked how Jamie was doing. We talked for a couple of minutes. Then, a curious question popped in my mind about how she was doing math with her 14-year-old. All at once, there was another question and another. The questions flowed one after another without my even thinking why I would be asking these things about homeschool. After all, I hadn't seen any angels lately! While listening to her, I glanced up on the wall and there were five precious faces staring back (my angels). They were my children and I knew then that I would be homeschooling them.   That was the answer. It was so clear. I was shocked; I could hardly finish talking to my friend. The emotion swelled up in my throat. I hung up and quickly called my husband and when I heard his voice I broke down in tears and said, "We're suppose to homeschool the kids!!" He said, "Okay...... (Pause)... Whatever you say!!" He was surprised, but immediately supportive. I cried the rest of the day!!   "I don't want to do this. It is too hard!", I would say to myself. "Briana's only 23 months and Kyla is only 4 months. I can't keep the laundry done or get the dinner on time as it is! How on earth can I do this!!", were the things that kept going through my mind. But there was an inner reassurance over and over again that I would be able to do it and that everything would be fine.

Notifying The School

This was in January and by April, I informed the school that my children would not be attending public school the next year and that we would be homeschooling them. The principal was so nice to us and said that she hated to see the Pierce children leave. She told me that she would get their records together. She also told me that if I ever needed anything, such as materials from the library or anything, to just call. I was very blessed to have this good experience leaving a public school to homeschool. However, I was prepared if there were to be a conflict. I knew Heavenly Father had directed me to do this and He would have helped me defend myself.

99

The Big GIANT Decision...Homeschool! By Penni Renee Pierce

A Confession

I need to tell you how "against" homeschooling I was. About 10 days before my big change of heart, my mother pulled my little brother, 14 years old, out of public school. He's like an only child, because he is the only one still living at home. I called my mother and told her that pulling David out was a bad mistake. I said it wasn't fair to David; that he was going to suffer socially. I was very adamant about how I felt. Mom was very calm. She told me, basically, thanks for being so concerned, but she knew what she was doing. Ten days later I was calling her to apologize and to say it is really none of my business to get mad about decisions she makes for David. And I told her I had been narrow minded and how sorry I was for not accepting and supporting her decision. Also, I had something to tell her. But, she guessed it before I said it. "You're going to homeschool the kids!" she said. "Yes, I'm going to do it." And I continued to tell her what had transpired. She was thrilled, to say the least!

No Fear

Well, that's it. That's how we got started in homeschool. From January until August of that year, I read everything I could get my hands on about homeschooling. I read more than I've ever read in my life! I knew, without a doubt, that I could do it. Now, I just had to make it a great homeschooling experience. The more I learned, the more any apprehension left me. "If you are prepared, you will not fear!!" ran over and over through my mind.

The Burden

Our decision to homeschool automatically solved some major worries. We ended up buying our home just three houses down from where we were leasing. Mark was five minutes from his work. "Which school district?" was no longer an issue. It felt like a huge burden had been lifted.

Children vs School Funding

Our son has asthma and in the first grade had been on about six different medications, including steroids. My mother had researched herbs and we took him off his medicine and put him on herbs and he is doing wonderfully (This should be done after consulting with a doctor).

Mark has been on herbs for about six years.   He was an "A", "B" student and had always made up all of his work from absences. It was such a comfort to think that we would not be dealing with the school and Mark's asthma absences again. His asthma attacks have been so few since we've begun homeschool. Let me tell you why they have lessened. Many of his attacks were triggered or made worse from the pressures at school. Then, when he would be absent, he would not only have his regular schoolwork to complete, but pounds and pounds more of all this "important stuff" he missed. And because of how self-conscious he is of his work being complete, this caused a tremendous amount of pressure on him. I was made to feel that they wanted my child at his desk no matter how bad he felt. Did you know funding is withheld from the public school for every day your child is absent? Mark was finally going to be free from the excessive amount of busy-work and the school district's rules and regulations about absentees!!!

No Time

It is also important to say that at some point in time, my children will be ready to leave home. I have six or seven years left with our oldest. That is not very long. I feel an urgency every day to make our time together important and fun. There are many necessary things for our children to learn before they leave home and our time is short.

Hurry Up And Learn This!

Most kids are under pressure at school. And some people may think homeschooling families are trying to protect their children or isolate them from "real life". Much of the atmosphere of public schools is taking away from their education. I feel the language that comes out of the mouths of children is totally out of control. My mother has always said, "The worst child abuse is raising your children so other people can't stand them!" The "uncalled for" behavior of students is contributing to a very negative environment. All children will ultimately enter the "real world" at one point or another. Why not take them while they are in their impressionable years and spend valuable <u>quantities</u> of time with them and help them to love learning about anything and everything in a positive, loving environment. Have you ever wondered how much of the 7-hour public school day your child spends watching the teachers discipline other people's ill-behaved children? There is a term I've heard among homeschoolers, it's "Detox". I was told my kids would go through "Public School Detoxification". They would be ridding themselves of a lot of negatives and pressure from the public school system. They would be cleansing themselves from the idea that "<u>all</u> learning occurs with due dates". The pressure of public school has stamped out the natural, burning desire to learn. Our ten-year-old once told me, "We always have to hurry at school; we never can make anything look nice!" She felt the pressure to move on to the next subject because they needed to "cover the whole book by the end of the year" or the need to move on because they "should have understood subtraction two days ago".

EXTRA NOTE: We have come a long way since that first year of homeschool. I wanted to note here that I don't like the word "detox". I feel that it is saying that everything about public school is wrong or poisonous. I don't

101

The Big GIANT Decision...Homeschool!   By Penni Renee Pierce

believe that. Besides this is not a book written to bash the public schools. This is hopefully a compiled work that testifies of other ways to successfully educate your children. The word "detox" could possibly be changed to the phrase "awakening the mind" to a realization that learning is possible at the kitchen table!

Do You Get It?

Many children do not feel good about school and, in particular, math, because they didn't "get it" in the third or fourth grades, but you can be sure the math book was finished by the end of the year! I have a 36-year-old sister who still breaks out in a cold sweat just to hear her child say, "I need help in MATH!" It doesn't have to be that way.

I do not believe in mathematics.

—Albert Einstein

NOTE: By the way, my sister Terri is 48 now. She still sweats about Math! However, she decided in the year 2000 to homeschool. She and her husband Vic have five boys and one girl. Their first two sons, Jared and Brad were finished with high school, so she homeschooled the other four. They now have three homeschool graduates, Bobby, John and Daniel. She is still homeschooling Abby and loving it. If Abby has a question, Terri just hands the math book to Vic.

Who Do You Blame?

When you think about it, how can teachers realistically help 30 children at their different levels of learning and understanding of math or any subject? Many students are left behind or just barely squeaking by on graduation day.   There are so many to blame; the teachers, the school principal, the school district, the parents, the people who write the textbooks, etc. I pray for the children and hope that they might be spared a lot of unnecessary anguish and stress.

There are also many talented and caring teachers. Much of their creativity and love of teaching has also been smothered because of the school districts fighting to keep up with one another, making unreasonable and unrealistic demands on the teachers.

Re-learning To Love Learning

Learning should be fun and interesting. There should be a desire in the student. I really did not think my 12-year-old daughter would ever like to read and this would be an ongoing problem. I never would have, ever, believed she would like history. My friend, Christie, kept telling me that Rachel would start loving to read in homeschool and she also said she had to tell her own kids to stop reading and get their chores done. She said her children asked for books for Christmas and birthdays. She said that they spend most of their Christmas money on books!! It was hardly believable. Trying to picture Rachel sitting in a chair and reading a book just for the mere joy of it was hard to imagine.

Reactions From Family and Friends

Let me tell you a few of the comments made when family and friends found that I would be homeschooling. To my surprise, everyone received the news with very positive attitudes. I really did care about what family members thought. My father-in-law was a little concerned about my ability to do it. But, he is very supportive and has helped the kids learn things about gardening and computers. He also saves science information from the newspaper for me. Everyone has been very supportive. My mother-in-law read *Homeschooling for Excellence* by David and Micki Colfax. She enjoyed it. Recommending books to family members might be a good way to help everyone be on the same "wavelength". Just about everyone I spoke to about our homeschooling either had a member of their family that was homeschooling or knew someone that homeschooled. Non-supportive family members can be a real obstacle to homeschooling families. You must pursue what you feel is best for your family, despite the negativity. However, always take family member's concerns very seriously and try to make them feel that you understand their worry and appreciate their concern. If you are doing a good job in homeschool, time will be your best friend.

If you find a path with no obstacles, it probably doesn't lead anywhere.
-Henry Wadsworth Longfellow

The Big Giant Responsibility

Here is something very interesting I witnessed. On my children's last day of public school, the responsibility for their education fell on my shoulders. I felt it. I knew it was there. But, guess who else felt it? My children. They were very concerned and excited about the books and materials they would be using. They questioned me to make sure I had thought of everything they would need. This was so exciting to see!!

We are taking a giant step forward to re-learn our love of learning. Homeschool is a big giant decision. It carries with it a big giant responsibility, but it is one I have come to happily accept.

EXTRA NOTE: Since I wrote the first edition, we are about to enter our 14th year of homeschooling. Mark, Rachel and Tahnee have graduated. Mark is 25 and married Christy. He went to community college, served a two year mission in Colorado and will be attending college in Columbia, Missouri graduating with a Civil Engineering Degree. Mark is very talented in math. Rachel is 23 and she married Eric. She attended community college and then went to BYU-Idaho with a scholarship. She is now a Registered Nurse and works in Postpartum and any other place they need her in the hospital. Tahnee graduated from homeschool and attended community college and then won an academic scholarship and went to BYU-Provo. She would like to be an interpreter and teach English as a second language.

104

The Big GIANT Decision...Homeschool!   By Penni Renee Pierce

Chapter 3
YES, I HAVE NO COLLEGE DEGREE
Your Credentials, Please!

Your Credentials, Please!

Many people have asked if I have a teaching degree and although I attended college the answer is NO. Then the question is if there is a college degree of any kind. NO. Being blessed, I did really well in school and in the one and a half years that I attended college, majoring in Early Childhood Education.

Once the decision to homeschool was made, the next thing to figure out was my own weaknesses. This was easy; HISTORY! I have never liked history, never!! I never cared about it. Every time I hear someone talk about history, I feel an uncontrollable urge to yawn. In my 11th grade year, my history teacher was also one of the football coaches. Everyday he would say, "Read the chapter and answer the questions." Everyday it was the same thing. He could have just recorded that sentence on a tape. Looking back on that class with a little bit of resentment, I realize that the coach/teacher either didn't know history and shouldn't have been there at all or he didn't care enough about any of us to teach us anything.

Despite a lot of the problems in public school, I lived through it. I was supplemented with help from parents and friends that understood what was going on. I had a lot of smart friends that helped me "get it".

So, besides history, all the other subjects in homeschool I felt I could handle, including math. Plus, if there is something complicated, there are lots of supportive people and places to get help.

Learning Friendly

That is the beauty of all the homeschool materials; they are made to be "learning friendly". Many of these materials are designed, especially for the homeschooler; whether it be math, language or science. Everything we have purchased so far has been very easy to follow. No guessing!! Teaching and learning are not technical procedures that need to be read about out of an 800 page text. Teaching and learning are very natural processes. And depending on the attitude of the teacher and student, great things can be accomplished.

With all that is available to homeschoolers, anyone can be successful. Anyone with the desire, that is.

Kindness and Understanding

Now, a few words about the teaching process- Maybe I'm not qualified to give this advice. Just take it as advice from someone who spent 12 years in public school and

13 years being a mother. *(EXTRA NOTE: And now 25 years being a mother and 13 years homeschooling!)* When you teach children, don't talk down to them, as if they were less of a person because they have only been on the earth 8 years. You can learn a lot from an 8-year-old!! When children don't understand a principle, such as a math principle, there is no point in getting upset or making them feel that they should be able to "get" this or that something is wrong with them. Put it away and do it again tomorrow!! They will eventually get it, but, only with a kind, understanding teacher and some time. I'm not giving this advice because I'm always kind and understanding; I'm giving it because I have made the mistakes and I know what works!

"Fellow Student"

Many people are under the impression that a homeschooling mother stands up in front of her children for seven hours and teaches. That is not the case. I am rarely standing up in front of my children to teach. Teaching occurs in many other ways. I love what Donn Reed says in his book, *The Home School Source Book* about the parent's role,

The parent plays several roles, the least of which is "teacher". The parent suggests, guides, converses, questions, supports, praises, encourages and helps to obtain material. The parent is friend, mentor, confidante and fellow student.

-Donn Reed
Author of The Home School Source Book

The Reward

At the beginning of our second year homeschooling, my son said, "I actually remember <u>all</u> the things we talked about and learned last year!" He was amazed that even though I had not had him memorize historical facts, he was able to recall all of his American history. We read and discuss our topics as we go and voice our opinions and feelings. These are our teaching moments.

"Yes, I have no college degree", but I am participating in my children's education in a very positive way.

You may have heard that old musician's joke: "Do you read music?" answer: "Yes, but not enough to hurt my pickin'!" Here it is as my mother tells it for homeschoolers: "Do you have a college education?" answer "Yes, but not enough to hurt my teachin'!"

106

The Big GIANT Decision...Homeschool!   By Penni Renee Pierce

Chapter 4
OUR DAILY SCHEDULE
Example Planning Sheets, To Have TV or Not To Have TV?

Planning Sheets

My friend got the idea for her daily planning sheets from attending a workshop by Beverly McCord at a homeschooling book fair. We have adopted this same idea for our homeschool. We use this sheet everyday and it helps keep us organized and focused. Our planning sheet has on it: Scripture Study, Math, Music, Grammar/Composition, Spelling, Reading, Science, History/Geography, Computer and Other.

EXTRA NOTE: After 13 years of homeschooling, we still use our daily planning sheets!

(Example of Daily Planning Sheet)

	MARK	RACHEL	TAHNEE
Scripture Study			
Math			
Music			
Grammar/Composition			
Spelling			
History/Geography			
Computer			
Reading			
Science			
Other			

We fill out a daily planning sheet everyday with the things we plan to do for that particular day. Then, the children check off the things they accomplished with a red pen. The kids like to check off what they did. All of the subjects will not be covered everyday. But, I have requirements, which are music, math, scriptures and reading, which must be done daily. These are the requirements my friend had for her children and this made sense, so we're copying her success. (Friends that have been homeschooling a while can help you tremendously!) There are three columns on the planning sheet for each of our three oldest children. So, there is always just one daily planning sheet used each day instead of a separate sheet for each child. This will cut down on paper work. We keep all of our daily planning sheets from the whole year in a notebook. This is a record of the children's participation in homeschool, an attendance record (because I write down right on the planning sheet if they were sick that day) and it shows that we are teaching the subjects required for our state. Also, if I ever had to prove to anyone that we were doing homeschool, this would be my record.

107

The Big GIANT Decision...Homeschool!   By Penni Renee Pierce

We have a weekly schedule that helps us to stick with things we would like to accomplish. Some people may like to be less structured than we are or some may think they want to be more rigid, but whatever you decide, just be flexible, because there will always be distractions.

(Example of a weekly schedule)

MONDAY	TUESDAY	WEDNESDAY	THURSDAY	FRIDAY
SCRIPTURES	SCRIPTURES	SCRIPTURES	SCRIPTURES	SCRIPTURES
MATH	MATH	MATH	MATH	MATH
MUSIC	MUSIC	MUSIC	MUSIC	MUSIC
HISTORY	HISTORY	HISTORY	HISTORY	HISTORY
LATIN	LANGUAGE	ANATOMY	LATIN	LANGUAGE
GEOGRAPHY	GRAMMAR	GRAMMAR	GRAMMAR	MUSIC/ART
GIVE SP. WORDS		SPELLING REVIEW	GEOGRAPHY	SPELLING TEST

Distractions

When we started our first week of homeschool, scripture study seemed to be the best subject to have first thing in the morning. It looked like a great way to start out the day. But, we were finding that the babies, who were 2 1/2 and 1 by that time, were a major distraction. They were waking up at different times in the morning and needing me to feed them and bathe them. Our 2 1/2-year-old went through a period of time where she would wake up first thing and start whining or crying. It was horrible for a while. I almost dreaded to hear her wake up. But, it has become increasingly better. If you have small children, your schedule must not be rigid. We didn't have scripture study and history in the morning anymore. It just wasn't working out. So, we grabbed our scriptures and history as soon as the 1-year-old went down for a nap. By that time, the 2 1/2-year-old was fairly content and was able to sit down and draw or look at books while we read aloud the scriptures and discussed American History. There were many times that we were interrupted with spilled milk, dirty diapers and anything else that could go wrong with a 1 and 2-year-old. But, somehow we were able to get our subjects done. We changed to doing math and music in the morning; that way the kids would come and ask me questions while I was caring for the babies. It worked out fine. Also, the daily planning sheets made life easier. Any special assignments could be written right on the daily planning sheet either the night before or early that morning. All the kids had to do was to read the planning sheet.

108

The Big GIANT Decision...Homeschool!   By Penni Renee Pierce

EXTRA NOTE: Our school schedule has changed many times over the past 13 years. At one point, we were even doing Math or writing at a certain time during the day, for example 9:30am math class begins. For one year, we also held school on Tuesdays, Wednesdays and Thursdays. That gave us a four-day weekend and we really concentrated our efforts on the three days of school. We accomplished a lot that year.

All Hours Are Learning Hours

Our school day starts at 8:00 am and usually finishes by 3:00 PM. There are some days when we finish by 2:00. However, there are many days that the kids work on homeschool, mostly reading or researching something, until 8:00 at night.

To Have TV, Or Not To Have TV?

A rule that we made when we started homeschool was that there would be no TV, except on Friday or Saturday. You would have thought I had announced a death in the family when I told them. But we have all adjusted. Plus, we get so much accomplished without the television.

EXTRA NOTE: As the kids got older, we started collecting movies. The kids really started enjoying many of the old movies. The only thing we watch on TV now is the news and weather. Anytime the TV is on, we have a movie in. We probably abuse that privilege sometimes too. However, Briana recently started writing a screen play and wants to produce it. She has already cast the parts with all of our extended family members. They are excited about doing it! Briana loves the 1940's, so naturally her story occurs in that era.

Pure Bliss!

Most of our days run smoothly. However, we do have our moments. Telling you that homeschooling is pure bliss would be inaccurate, of course. If you can picture our 13-year-old son tapping his pencil on the table while our 10-year-old daughter is trying to do math. And our son loving every minute of tormenting her!! This is just part of life.

Desks? What Are Those?

I have to say that we have wonderful children, but there are a few things we are striving to achieve. Such as, learning when and when not to tease. Or, trying to complete our assignments in a timely manner. In our first year of homeschooling we definitely learned our weaknesses. And we are constantly trying to figure out how to make life easier. Sometimes it works better for everyone to be in separate rooms to do math.

109

The Big GIANT Decision...Homeschool!   By Penni Renee Pierce

But, for the most part, we are all together. Rachel, our 12-year-old, likes to do most of her work in her room by herself. There is less distraction from the little ones. We have desks in the kids' rooms, but they tend to migrate to the dining room or the couch. I'm not picky about where they do their work as long as it gets accomplished and they're not bothering one another.

EXTRA NOTE: Our youngest, Kyla is now 13 and Rachel is a college graduate.

Math-Honesty-Cheating

We try to get up by 7:00 am and be started by 8:00 am. The kids do their math first. We use *Saxon Math* and they are all on different levels. They all are required to do one lesson a day and check it and tell me about any missed problems and why. We have talked with our children many, many times about honesty since they were tiny. We have never had a problem with cheating. If we had a child we thought would be tempted with this, we would handle the checking of papers in a totally different way. This is something you would have to evaluate in your own situation. Anyway, checking is a great way for kids to reinforce their understanding quickly after they have completed their work.

Recess! My Favorite Subject!

Everyday at about 10:00 am we go outside and play. The kids ride their bikes, roller-skate, jump rope, run races or just sit in the sun and talk. We usually stay out for at least 30 to 45 minutes. We come back in and they finish up anything they were working on, then they eat lunch. Later we work on grammar, creative writing, reading, etc.

Social Life

Many people feel that homeschoolers are isolated and are not being socially fed. Most of the socialization that goes on at school is negative and I'm thankful our children are not around it day in and day out. Rachel is involved in a ballet class, Tahnee is on a soccer team and Mark was on an "all homeschoolers" baseball team last year. They are all involved in youth groups at church and have activities once a week. Mark and Rachel are also at the age where they are doing odd jobs, such as mowing lawns and baby sitting. In these jobs, they are dealing with adults and negotiating their pay. They are definitely not socially deprived.

110

The Big GIANT Decision...Homeschool! By Penni Renee Pierce

Born-a-Homeschooler

Briana, our 3-year-old wants to be totally involved in homeschool. She would see the kids doing Math and say, "Mom, where's MY math book?" I fixed a notebook for her that says "Briana's Math". We put stickers on some of the pages in groups of 2's, 3's, 4's, etc., so that she can practice counting them. She also has a journal that she "writes" in while the other kids are writing in their journals. Kyla, our 2-year-old likes to write with a pencil or pen. We give her paper and pencil whenever she asks. We also have many, many books for Kyla and Briana. I try to make a point to spend time everyday reading with them or the older kids read to them. Briana loves to tell me the story of *Green Eggs and Ham* while she is pretending to read from the book. Her story is surprisingly accurate. As soon as a child shows interest in anything, try to involve them. Of course, involve them at their own level of understanding so that they feel successful.

> *Briana is 3 and while reading to her today she stopped
> me and said, "Books grow on trees." I am sure I had a
> confused look on my face. I checked the pictures to see if there were
> any fruit or trees we were reading about. The book was
> about a cat. I said, "Did you say BOOKS grow on trees?"
> She said, "Yes, books grow on trees." Then I remembered that
> we had a discussion a few weeks earlier about how paper was made!
> So she had come to her own conclusion that
> BOOKS GROW ON TREES!*

One Teacher- Five Students

We get many things done in our homeschool day. It is great having one teacher for five students! Our scheduling has had to be very flexible, but we are learning what works. And as the little ones get older, our schedule will change again and again. Daily schedules are important and it is beneficial to have one to do homeschool. This way everyone knows what is expected of them.

EXTRA NOTE: Now that Mark, Rachel and Tahnee have graduated from homeschool, we are just homeschooling Briana and Kyla. Briana is 15 and Kyla is 13. Briana and Kyla have never been to public school. They are doing Algebra. They are excellent readers and do very well at creative writing. Those are the three things that I focus on the most. Along with piano practice too!

111

The Big GIANT Decision...Homeschool! By Penni Renee Pierce

Chapter 5
MATH NOTES
Math Principles, Kitchen Math, Math Intimidation, etc.

Grades

There are correspondence schools and homeschool companies that offer pre-packaged curricula. In other words, you order everything you need for your 4th grader all in one package. We would rather have more control over what we get, so we have chosen to find things we enjoy as we go. We do not give grades for anything, except math and spelling. I have the kids keep an average of their math test grades.

Saxon Math

We use the *Saxon Math* program. We put our 9-year-old in the *Saxon* 54, which is an advanced 4th grade or average 5th grade math book. It was moving a little too fast after about lesson 40. So, I went to the library and checked out a 3rd grade math book. We reviewed the entire book for the rest of the year. We are continuing *Saxon* 54 now in our second year of homeschool and she is doing great. However, as I write this book, the *Saxon* K-3rd have become available for homeschoolers at a reasonable price through *Love To Learn* (see the **Catalogs and Materials** section of this book). Some veteran homeschoolers have had much success with starting their children in *Developmental Math* and then working up to *Saxon* 54. Both of these math programs can also be purchased through *The Always Incomplete Resource Guide and Catalog* (See **Catalogs and Materials** section in this book).

Math Principles

I spent a lot of one-on-one with our 9-year-old in math and will continue this. Because she is at a very critical age where she is still learning many of the basic principles that she <u>must</u> grasp to be able to continue in higher math. I also help Mark and Rachel with their questions and also with any confusion they have had about basic principles. Mark sometimes helps Rachel. This is great for building his confidence. Sometimes they have to refresh my memory about a principle before I can answer their question. I have discovered many holes in my own education this past year!! How fun it has been filling those holes!

Extra Math Fun

We have purchased the triangle flash cards, fraction bars and **Number Jumbler** as extra fun things for math. We also used ideas from the book *Family Math* by Jean Kerr Stenmark, Ruth Cossey and Virgina Thompson. This is a fun book of math games and introduces new ways of thinking about numbers!

112

The Big GIANT Decision...Homeschool!   By Penni Renee Pierce

Kitchen Math

I have always had a tendency to help my children with everything. My husband insists that I must let them try to do things on their own. Then, if they need help, I should help. So, one of the things I am having them learn is how to cook. Mark and Rachel can both go in the kitchen, read a recipe and follow it and even double it without assistance. They use math quite a bit in the kitchen. The kitchen is a wonderful learning area without them even realizing.

Math Intimidation

Math can be intimidating to some parents, but I think if you learn along with your children, it will help. You will see areas you didn't understand when you were in school and be able to get those straightened out. My kids are helping me memorize the multiplication tables, which I never memorized. I still have to stop and think about the answer to 6 x 7. Rachel and I are learning percentages together. It is really helping me to reinforce a few points that weren't clear to me in school. I made "A's" in Algebra II in high school, but I still find many gaps in my understanding and being able to recall some basic principles.

Grasping the Concepts

Saxon Math is very self-explanatory and repetitive. If you miss something on a test, you can figure out right away where you misunderstood the concept. And the great thing is that the child is under no pressure to go on to the next math concept, until they grasp the one upon which they're working.

Stop And Learn It!

When Tahnee, our 9-year-old, had reached the multiplication tables, we stopped doing anything else in the text book and just worked on multiplication. When we went back to the book about a week later, she commented how easy all the work in the text seemed since she had really studied and practiced her multiplication tables.

Review Before Moving On!

Our first year of homeschool, Mark would have been in the 7th grade. I wasn't sure his understanding of some of the math concepts were clear. So, I started him in *Saxon 76*, which is right before pre-algebra. He informed me that it was way too easy for him. So, he started taking all the tests for that level (to see if he could test-out of that book). If he did well on those tests he could go on to pre-algebra, which is called Algebra 1/2 in the *Saxon* program. To my surprise, instead of just taking each test and checking it, he read each lesson to make sure he understood each principle being taught for that section. Then, he took the tests. Also, as he read the lessons, if there

113

The Big GIANT Decision...Homeschool! By Penni Renee Pierce

was something of which he was not sure, he would do the practice problems for that principle, then take the test. I did not tell him to do it this way. He took this upon himself. Like I said earlier, our kids have really felt the responsibility for their own education.

Self-Motivation

One day Rachel was not understanding the formula for figuring the area of some various shapes. She went to the back of her book and found some extra practice problems for figuring area. She didn't finish her regular math work during our school time, because she had spent time learning that principle and doing the extra practice. That night she got out her regular math work for that day and finished it. I didn't assign this to her. She could have completed it the next day, as far as I was concerned. But she is learning to be responsible and self-motivated.

It's All In The Attitude

I have heard that employers like to hire homeschoolers because the homeschooled children have respect, initiative, and self-motivation. I really believe it since I've seen our children this past year and their attitude about learning.

Curricula Flexibility

Math was a concern before I started homeschool, but *Saxon Math* has made it possible to pin point any problem areas. I'm sure there are other good homeschool math programs. *Saxon* has worked for us, so far. But, I'm very flexible and if I see something I like better or think would be beneficial for a particular child, I would change to that. However, once you have chosen a curriculum, stick to it for a while to make sure it will work or not. Everyone that does homeschool should be very open to the possibility of making a wrong curricula choice. You can't beat yourself up over it. Just go on and talk to others doing homeschool and read and you'll find things that will work for you.

EXTRA NOTE: Since our first year, we have also used Developmental Math before Saxon or for extra practice. Also, we have used Math-It for the drills. But, ultimately we use Saxon all the time still.

Chapter 6
HISTORY NOTES
Time Lines, Globes, Biographies, Lemon Juice Documents

Naps During History

As soon as our 1-year-old went down for a nap, we studied our scriptures and American History. I read aloud out of the scriptures and the kids would ask questions as we went along.

Two Time Lines

For American History, we made a time line out of white butcher paper we purchased at Walmart. The kids would record scriptural events and events from American History. This is a very good learning tool for them. Sometimes, while reading aloud about William Penn, for example, they would be marking the date on the time line. Also, each of the children had a notebook with dividers. Each divider has a year, such as "1400's", "1500's", "1600's", etc. As we discussed different events in history they would also record it in their time line book. I found the time line book idea from a catalog called *The Always Incomplete Resource Guide and Catalog* by Bob and Tina Farewell. This catalog is a "must have" for homeschoolers. They sell a book in their catalog called *Book of the Centuries* by Bonnie Dettmer. This is where the idea for time line books was found. You might ask why we would do a time line and a time line book. When I was in school I didn't have an understanding for history and dates. If our children had a time line to look at on the wall, plus a time line book to use as a reference, this might help them have a good picture of when things occurred in history.

EXTRA NOTE: We are doing a timeline with Briana and Kyla that is created on banner paper. It is fan folded so that it can be completely unfolded to view the whole thing or you can just view 100 years at a time on one page. I am having them write in familiar dates.

Whatever Strikes Our Interest

I chose *A Child's Story of America* by Michael J. Mchugh and Dr. Charles Morris as our American History guideline. This is read aloud to the children. Then, if there is something that strikes our interest, we study all about that area or subject. For example, we studied about Christopher Columbus. We found out some things about his character, his father, his country and his talents. We have found it to be very interesting to read from several sources about events in history.

A Tool-The Globe

We looked up continents or cities on the globe whenever we came across them in our reading. The globe is a very valuable tool.

Places and Ships

We studied about the beginning of Jamestown and the Pilgrims. We looked up information about the Mayflower and how it was built and what became of it. The children made a 5 foot long "Pilgrim Banner" that showed the pilgrim voyage across to America, their common houses they built, the dimensions of the Mayflower, the friendly Indians and even the purpose of the Mayflower Compact.

People

We studied about the Dutch, the Quakers and William Penn, also General James Oglethorpe.

Indians, Indians and More Indians

We studied all about the American Indians, probably over a month's time. We read all kinds of books from the library such as *Sequoyah, Wilma Mankiller, The Blackfoot*, and many, many more. We even had a "Power History Day" where we learned about American Indians all day. We read about them; we learned a little Cherokee language; we made pemmican (an Indian food for long journeys); we made Indian crafts with leather; the children wrote papers about how they felt the Indian land problem should have been handled and we made and played authentic native American games. The kids still talk about the American Indians. They love "Power History Day"!! They beg all the time for another "Power Day" (See Power Days chapter).

Daniel Boone

We also read about Daniel Boone's life out of *The Childhood of Famous Americans* series (some titles from this series are still out-of-print). Even with our children being all different ages, they loved this book. They admired Daniel Boone after reading this and many parts in the book were funny!!

Colonial Days

We have also read books about the Colonial times. The kids really enjoyed learning about how people lived from Ann McGovern's *If You Lived in Colonial Times* book. We also used an Edwin Tunis' book *Colonial Living* as a resource. The kids made posters of and wrote reports about the Colonial era.

116

The Big GIANT Decision...Homeschool! By Penni Renee Pierce

Historical Biographies

We read about *Paul Revere and the Minute Men* by Dorothy Canfield Fisher which is an out-of-print Landmark Book. We learned many things about Paul Revere of which I had never heard. We collect the Landmark books at library sales and other book sales or half price book stores. I usually pay $1.00 to $2.00 per book, but have paid as much as $6.00 for one of my Landmarks. You can also contact Lifetime Books and Gifts to see if they have any available, but you will pay a bit more for them (see **Catalogs and Materials** for more information). Landmark books are very good history books.

Lemon Juice Documents

We also collect the *Cornerstone of Freedom* series and we read *The Declaration of Independence* from this series. It was very good. The kids got out their thesaurus and renamed the Declaration of Independence. Each one of them came up with a name that this famous historical document could have been called. For example: "Proclamation of Liberation". We typed the new names into the computer and printed each one out in a script font. To make the paper look old, we painted it with lemon juice and placed it on a cookie sheet. We put it in the oven on broil, on the rack furthest from the heat (you have to watch it close!). After it turned brown, we took it out and burned the edges with a candle (by the way, burning the edges is dangerous; I did it myself with a candle in the kitchen sink, so that it could be dropped in the sink if needed. Burn only a little bit at a time and keep blowing it out, then re-lighting it.) We displayed our lemon juice documents at our Open House at the end of the year.

A Lost Story In History

In history, we also studied about the Acadians, whom I had never learned about when I was in school. It was very interesting! The kids really enjoyed hearing this story and discussing it. I previewed the Landmark book *Evangeline and the Acadians* by Robert Tallant. It tells about the history of the Acadians and also about a poem Henry Wadsworth Longfellow wrote about an Acadian woman. I checked out the poem "Evangeline" from the library and we studied all 50 to 60 pages of it with my friend Christie and her children. We looked up probably about 200 or more vocabulary words. The kids loved this story and understood it and we were able to mix vocabulary, literature and history all together. This was probably one of the highlights of our first year in homeschool.

A Book With A Good Reputation

We are reading another Landmark book called *The American Revolution* by Bruce Bliven, Jr.(This book happens to still be in print, in paperback.) The kids are enjoying it and are asking some very thought provoking questions. The reason we seek after

The Big GIANT Decision...Homeschool! By Penni Renee Pierce

117

the out-of-print Landmark books is because of the high moral standards they uphold. They are well written and make history come to life.

Give It A Chance!

I worked hard to begin our first year with a very positive and enthusiastic outlook toward history. I didn't want any of the negative feelings I had about history to show through and give my kids the wrong impression. I really wanted to give history a chance, just as I wanted my children to give history a chance. Since we've completed our first year of homeschool, if you ask us our favorite subject, we all say-   HISTORY!

118

The Big GIANT Decision...Homeschool!   By Penni Renee Pierce

Chapter 7
LANGUAGE NOTES
Creative Writing, Spelling, Reading, Poetry, Reading Aloud, etc.

Easy Grammar

For language, we purchased *Easy Grammar* by Wanda C. Phillips for Mark and Rachel (12 and 11 years old at that time). I really like the way this book introduces prepositions first. If the kids can pick out all the prepositional phrases in a sentence, then they will be able to easily identify the other parts of speech.

We also bought *Daily Grams* green workbook by the same author, which we did not use yet. Mark and Rachel just worked out of the *Easy Grammar* workbook.

We did grammar quite a bit in our first year but, if there was something else we needed to work on, such as literature or spelling, we worked on that and grammar would take a backseat. Grammar is important to understand, but it is not "super high" on my priority list. For example, getting into diagramming sentences. I loved learning this in school, but I never used it again, ever!

EXTRA NOTE: For Briana and Kyla, I used the Easy Grammar program starting in 8th and 9th grades.

Language Arts

For our 9-year-old, we purchased *Learning Language Arts through Literature* by Dr. Ruth Beechick. I've really enjoyed doing this with Tahnee. The excerpts are used from famous literature. Also, there are many areas covered that kids really need to know; for example, how to use a phone book, prefixes, suffixes, writing paragraphs and much more. We were so pleased with this program that we bought it for Mark and Rachel. While writing this book, we have already begun our second year of homeschool and this language program is working out beautifully for Mark and Rachel.

EXTRA NOTE: I will be using ideas from Learning Language Arts Through Literature for Briana and Kyla. Also, Rachel mentioned the dictation part was very helpful to her later when taking notes in college class. In the Learning Language Arts Through Literature program there are lessons that are dictated from classics or the scriptures. The student must write what you speak. This is great to develop listening skills.

119

The Big GIANT Decision...Homeschool!   By Penni Renee Pierce

Creative Writing

Dorothy Rich's book *Megaskills* will give you some ideas on how to teach writing. I love her "writing umbrella" idea, where you teach children to write a paragraph and they learn to stay on the subject. It's fun!!

I also have various workbooks and books on teaching writing skills or creative writing to children that I have picked up at teacher supply stores or book sales. One of the ideas from these workbooks was an assignment like this: "Pick an event from American History and tell it from an animal's point of view; for example, Paul Revere's horse. What was this animal feeling and thinking about during this historical event?" Also, we read aloud "The Emperor's New Clothes" and then the kids picked their favorite fairy tale and wrote a "Fractured Fairy Tale" by telling basically the same story, but with different characters or modernizing it. Mark's title was "The President's New Saxophone".

There are writing programs available for homeschoolers, such as *Complete Writing Lessons for Primary Grades or Middle Grades* by Marjorie Frank or *Easy Writing* by Wanda C. Phillips and there are more. I have not purchased a structured writing program. We have done fine the first year without it. However, I will always be reading about what is available in case it is necessary to be more structured in this area. The book *If You're Trying to Teach Kids To Write, You've Gotta Have This Book* by Marjorie Frank, will help YOU with the right attitude about writing. There are so many ideas in this book. It is fantastic!!

EXTRA NOTE: For Briana and Kyla, I have made up my own creative writing prompts to help them get started on a paper. Also, I have found "free" creative writing prompts to print from the internet.

A Reason For Writing

The kids also keep journals. Rachel and Tahnee really enjoyed writing in their journals. However, Mark does not enjoy it at all. Even though his first few entries in his journal were very well written, he couldn't see a reason for writing. But, I wanted him to write everyday, anything! I think I may have been a little too strict about him writing. I finally realized my pressure was not helping. Reluctantly, I told him to forget about the journal writing. After much thought, I told him to write about all the inventions he thinks up and describe them. He was describing a new invention to me every day, so if he kept track of them by writing them down, it would be fun to look back on, plus he was writing! I also purchased a book for kids about being an inventor and getting things patented. It is called *How To Be An Inventor* by Murray Suid. So, he started writing about several things he would like to invent. This was a great way to get him writing. By the way, Mark's paper, on the historical event from an animal's point of view, was

120

The Big GIANT Decision...Homeschool!   By Penni Renee Pierce

fantastic. He loved this activity. He told me, for the first time ever, he was really proud of something he had written. As talented as he is, I'm not sure why writing is a hard task for him. He needs a cause and maybe an experience to which he can relate. Lately, however, Mark has been attaining a natural desire to put ideas into writing. Kids need an idea in which they're interested and lots of time with no pressure and they'll have some great things to put down on paper.

We also started a garden this year and are keeping a garden journal. Just in case any veggies turn out extra good, we'll know what we did!! This also teaches the kids the value of keeping a record that we may need to refer to later. They will really get the picture of this next year when we get out the journal before we plant the new garden.

Spelling

We also had spelling tests this year. We gathered all our spelling words from what we were reading; for example scriptures, history or the kids own personal reading. This made the spelling words have more meaning, not just a random list of words. Sometimes the kids would all have separate lists, but sometimes everyone had the same list of words. We would discuss their meanings and usage. Sometimes they would write the words five times each or in sentences. They would also drill each other the night before the test. Also, the night before the test, I would record, on a cassette tape, their spelling tests. That way, they could take their test the next day whenever it was convenient for them.

Latin

We are also very excited about a program called *English From the Roots Up* by Joegil Lundquist. This is supposed to help with reading, writing, spelling and S.A.T. scores. This is a Latin course. It is very simple to use and incorporate into your curriculum. I had Latin in high school, but I wish I had had a course like this in elementary school. It is amazing how many Latin and Greek roots we use everyday and how it ties in with all subjects. Investigating this program for your children would be worth the time.

Turned On To Reading

At the beginning of our homeschool year, the only rule I made about reading was that the kids pick out a book and read out of it everyday. This was very easy for our 12 and 9-year-olds. But, for our 11-year-old it was hard. She just didn't like to read. Finally, we talked her into choosing a Bill Wallace book.

A few years ago our son also disliked reading. At that time, I went to the library and saw a Bill Wallace book called *Danger in Quicksand Swamp*. I read it myself. I loved it and said to Mark, "You have to read this book. You will not be able to put it down!!"

He read it and thereafter read all the Bill Wallace books and more. He was completely turned on to reading. So, we thought Rachel might get hooked if she read a Bill Wallace book. She read *Danger on Panther Peak*. It took her a while and she was so happy that she had read a book all the way through. She cared more about reading an entire book than what the story was about. She found another book by Bill Wallace called *Beauty*. She absolutely loved it. She loves horses and this was about a horse. After that book, there was no stopping her. She has now read so many books I can't even list them all. Rachel, however, will list books she has read in her book review in the back of this book. My friend was right; I have to make her put the books down to do other things. To me, this has truly been a miracle. Thank you, my friend Christie for your reassurance and you too, Bill Wallace!!!

Before Rachel gained this love of reading, I had her read aloud to me first to make sure that her dislike for reading wasn't a fundamental problem. If she had had a problem with understanding how to read, we would have tackled that problem first before encouraging her to read lengthy amounts of material. Her love of reading occurred because there was no pressure of getting it done by a certain date. There were no assigned book reports. However, all the kids are giving me underlined, oral book reports all the time. They love telling me about what they have read and answering my questions.

A 16-year-old homeschooler told me recently
that he never wanted to read until he started homeschooling
three years ago. Every time I see him now he
has a book in his hand!

EXTRA NOTE: As college students, Mark, Rachel and Tahnee gave some valuable advice. They told me that I needed to do more reading comprehension with Briana and Kyla because every community college entrance test has reading comprehension on it. So, I found a reading comprehension program that uses excerpts from classic novels. I really have liked the *Bring the Classics to Life* series, published by Edcon. You can order these from www.edconpublishing.com.

Reading and Communicating

Our 9-year-old read *Charlotte's Web*, the *Ramona* series, the *Pee Wee Scout* series and now she's reading The *Little House on the Prairie* series. She loves reading.

Mark, our 12-year-old read the *Hobbit*, two of the *Lord of the Rings* books, *Little House on the Prairie*, Lloyd Alexander series and C.S. Lewis series.

I read the *Hobbit* also this past year. This has been a great source of communication between Mark and me. I would encourage parents to read their children's books. It will create unity between you and your children. I also read the *Little House in the Big Woods* while my 9-year-old read it too. It was so fun to discuss it with her. I could never keep up with reading every book they read, but a few favorites here and there are a great way to keep up with things they are learning and feeling.

You Mean I Have To READ The Instructions?!

Mark has also checked out card trick books and read some pretty complicated instructions and followed them. I've also noticed he is not inhibited by any kind of game instructions. This is very important for kids to know. Teach them the value of reading instructions!!

Reading Aloud

I read aloud to the kids everyday. We read our scriptures and history. We read *Heidi* this past year and then went to see the community theater play of "Heidi". The kids loved it! Reading aloud to your children helps them to use their imaginations. It helps them to listen to words instead of seeing it written in front of them. Plus, you will have things to discuss and other activities will be spontaneously created, such as, creative writing papers written from your history lesson or a unit study on American Indians.

Poetry

As I had mentioned in the History chapter, we studied the poem *Evangeline* by Henry Wadsworth Longfellow. We first discussed some history of the Acadians. Then we talked about Longfellow's life. We took the poem *Evangeline* and highlighted all the words the kids didn't know, which were over 200 words. We looked up all the definitions then read the poem aloud and discussed it. Our 11 and 12-year-old enjoyed it. We lost our 9-year-old's attention quite a bit. But, later on Tahnee and I had our own private discussion of *Evangeline*. She would ask, "Now, what happened in *Evangeline* today?" She loved the story when I told it to her in my own words.

Wow!

Reading together and discussing characters has really strengthened our children's fluency of language and comprehension skills.

Our kids have changed their priority list for Christmas and birthdays. They want books! They talk about books, they critique books and they want to own books!!

Chapter 8
SCIENCE NOTES
Rock Candy, Monkeys, The Creation

Rock Candy

We did a rock and mineral unit this year for science. The kids wrote reports on diamonds, rocks and volcanoes. They really enjoyed this. We found a book that had many questions about rocks. Then, the book answers the questions and gives examples. This book is called *Answers About Rocks and Minerals* by Frederick Smithline. I prepared a list of these questions for each person. Then, we tried answering them without the book. The kids did a couple of rock experiments and we made rock candy. To top it off, the civic center had a rock and mineral show that happened to be at the same time we were studying rocks. The rock show was wonderful. It was great for the kids to see some rock samples we had talked about. We are also planning a trip to the Diamond Mine in Arkansas.

Monkeys

Tahnee became very interested in monkeys this year. She read several books, some of which I would have thought above her reading level. But she read them and told me about monkeys in detail. She also wrote an excellent report and drew some very detailed pictures of what she liked about monkeys. I did not give this assignment. She just did it on her own.

Science And The Creation

There is a really interesting and fun way to teach science, which I learned about from reading the *Always Incomplete Resource Guide and Catalog* by Bob and Tina Farewell (See **Catalogs and Materials** section in this book).   In this catalog, a lady named Tricia Folker of Leesburg, Florida, had an overview of her science program taught according to the days of the creation. Each day representing an area of science; for instance, Day 1 is Physics and Day 6 is Earth, Zoology and Man. If you use this overview, you will be covering all areas of science. It's wonderful! Also, the catalog has taken each science area and given you many books to choose from at different age levels.

Here are some of the books I've purchased after reading about this science overview; *Chemically Active* by Vicki Cobb, *Simple Science Experiments with Everyday Materials* by Muriel Mandell. The last book even gives some historical facts. For example, "What is a straw? Who patented it and when was the first straw-making machine invented?" This book is very interesting. We've also purchased *The Usborne Book of Science, An introduction to Biology, Physics, and Chemistry*, a great resource book. *Blood and Guts* by Linda Allison is a great book especially for kids interested in how the body really

124

The Big GIANT Decision...Homeschool!   By Penni Renee Pierce

works! It has some wonderful activities for all ages. We also bought for each child the Dover Coloring books called *Human Anatomy*. We also invested in some colored pencils with a large color variety to use with these coloring books.   These pencils may be a little more expensive than your regular colored pencils, but it is worth it.   The coloring books include a great text about the human body.

On the creation overview, Tricia puts for Day 7: Rest, for which we bought a book called *Celebrate the Feasts* by Martha Zimmerman.   This book tells all about the different feasts from the Old Testament and why they were celebrated and how to teach about these celebrations to your family and it even gives some recipes of dishes used in the celebration.   This may have nothing to do with science, but I like the way she included a day of rest in her overview. Also, your day of rest could include a trip to the zoo, planetarium or natural history museum.

EXTRA NOTE: We have spent most of our "science" time going to science museums or reading about science. I love to spend some of our summer time playing science games and doing more in depth study of the body or other science things. I feel that if my children really want to be scientists, they can study more in college. With that in mind, our son Mark ended up with a talent in math and physics and Rachel went into the medical profession!

Being There
Charlotte Mason, an educator who lived in the mid 1800's to early 1900's believed that children need to enjoy nature by being directly in it! Take your children to a park, the beach, the countryside, a stream, etc. Talk about the things you see. This is a child's best experience with science; *being there* and seeing it. (This activity is not just for little ones of course, but, for all children of all ages.)

> *My mother and 15-year-old brother, David, were walking down the dirt road on their farm. David was quiet for a while. Then he asked, "I wonder if all the messages being sent through the Internet are affecting the weather patterns?" My mom's answer, "Good question!"*

EXTRA NOTE: David is now 27 years old. He served a two year mission in the Netherlands. He married Amy and just finished his bachelors degree in business and computer technology. He is brilliant with computers and anything technical. He also loves to invent things!

Chapter 9
GEOGRAPHY NOTES
Homemade Game, Languages & Countries, Globes, Maps, etc.

Loving Geography

This is a hard area for me to teach since geography was not my best subject in school. There is a book called *Hands-On Geography* by Maggie S. Hogan and Janice Baker. This has "Easy and Fun Activities for Exploring God's World". We did one of the activities for the summer. We wanted to learn about Egypt. We went and checked out about 40 books about Egypt from our public library. The kids gathered 10 questions each about Egypt and put them on index cards. Then we put white paper over the top of an old game board that we never used. They drew a new game board on this white paper. It is very elaborate with a huge King Tut mask in the center with Egyptian drawings along the edges. Then, of course, spaces to move along. They did a wonderful job and it is a very fun way to learn about Egypt or any other country for that matter. This is just one of the many fun activities from this geography book. We also made maps of Egypt and labeled them and used colored pencils to color them. I also purchased a book called *In Search of King Tut's Tomb* illustrated by the Brothers Hildebrandt. I bought this through a Discovery Toys representative. The illustrations are beautiful. There are lots of geographical and historical tid bits. It is a Hide and Seek Puzzle Book and we have enjoyed doing this together.

Foreign Language- Where is the country?

Also, for Geography, I purchased *Words for the World* by Christine Ege. This is a collection of tapes and a hardbound book that introduces eight countries and their languages. We are very excited about doing this series.

Globes, Maps, Plan A Trip

Of course, we also have a globe and large maps for the wall. Rand McNally puts out a travel map for children. I saw one at our discount bookstore and it was very colorful and looked like a fun way to introduce map reading or plan a trip.

One homeschooling family I know, fills in a blank map of the United States and a blank map of the continents every day, until everyone knows it. This would be a fun way to start, then you could increase the difficulty of the map.

EXTRA NOTE: We still use the fill-in-the-blank maps with Briana and Kyla.

126

The Big GIANT Decision...Homeschool! By Penni Renee Pierce

Chapter 10
COMPUTER NOTES
Dinosaurs, Keyboard Tutor, Beware Of Software

Dinosaurs

In 1984, my husband purchased two Osborne computers (You may have heard of these dinosaurs!). They were compact with the screen being approximately 6" x 6". This was my first experience with computers. The typewriter seemed superior, to me. (After all, it had a carriage return and the computer did not!) But, once the computer was given a chance, it beat the typewriter by far. These Osbornes were used for the next two years to type medical reports, which made it possible for me to make enough money to pay our rent and stay at home with the children. Mark was working two part-time jobs and going to school.

Keyboard Tutor

I was 24 years old when introduced to computers. Most 3-year-olds can boot up a computer these days. Computers should not be an option when considering homeschool. You must have one in your home. Even if it is an older one; at least the kids can get use to the computer and become familiar with the keyboard. I strongly recommend some sort of typing or keyboard tutor software for your children to learn to type correctly. Our children use a typing tutor about 3 to 5 times per week.

Beware Of Software

There is so much available for the computer. There are educational software and games for the computer, too. Use caution when purchasing software. There is a lot of unwholesome material. When we bought our new computer, it came with some "free" games and some of these were "rated" because of violence and language.

Time

Also, use caution about time spent on the computer. Use the computer as a tool and in moderation. Obviously, in our world today the kids have to be computer literate. But, kids waste hours and hours with games (as do some adults)! Don't fool yourself into thinking, "if they're using the computer, it must be educational!"

SAT/ACT

As you may have realized by now, I do not think highly of standardized testing. However, by the time the children are entering their high school years, they must start thinking about their SAT and ACT testing (unfortunately the measuring stick of our society). Software is available for these two tests which will help your children

127

The Big GIANT Decision...Homeschool! By Penni Renee Pierce

study and take sample tests. This will help them understand which skills are tested and how to take these tests. There will be much less anxiety on test day.

Somewhere There's Somebody

Don't let the "computer age" intimidate you. Your kids won't be intimidated at all!! There is always someone around, somewhere to answer a computer question and of course there's always the software manuals to read, ha ha!! So, if you do not have a computer, figure out a way to get one. Save, save, save!

EXTRA NOTE: I have found that the internet has come a long way over the past 13 years. Our family has found many, many things we want to study or order because of the internet. We have observed Hailey's Comet, walked through King Tut's tomb, toured the White House, etc. It is amazing the places you can see on the internet without traveling!

128

The Big GIANT Decision...Homeschool! By Penni Renee Pierce

Chapter 11
PHYSICAL EDUCATION NOTES
What about P.E.?

What about P.E. in homeschool? I do not have fond memories of P.E. in public school. Some of the locker room scenes were not real positive! There is a feeling of relief that my kids are not going to be around this. As far as physical education goes and I stress the word EDUCATION, I'm all for it! I really believe that teaching our children to be active and knowledgeable about health is one of the greatest lessons we can give to them. I also believe that sports can help children understand what it means to be a part of a team, not to mention the fun of playing a particular sport. Our children are involved in sports and dance. We talk about good health with them. My husband and I exercise everyday and they see this. We see them using our hand weights sometimes and wanting to go jogging with us. Our YMCA has a physical education class for homeschoolers. It costs $80.00 per child. So that would cost us $240.00 for P.E. Boy, that must be some P.E. class! We have not invested in this so far. But, it's nice to know it is available. As for now, our physical education is playing and exercising together as a family and going to the kid's sporting and dance events.

EXTRA NOTE: Briana and Kyla have taken a couple of dance classes over the past years. Their favorite was Irish dancing. They both have bicycles that they ride. We go for walks. They play basketball, volleyball and softball here in our little town sometimes and they play sports at church.

Kites rise highest against the wind – not with it.
–Sir Winston Churchill

Chapter 12
POWER DAYS
Power Math, Power History, Power Music, etc.

Power Days are like a unit study. We study about one area for an entire day, like math, for example. Sometimes, you may need to take two days for this to complete everything. I made up the title "Power Day" because we were going to have more brain power in that subject by the end of the day, hopefully! These are some things we did:

Power Math Day
* Think of every word you can that has to do with math
*We took all these words and alphabetized them and taped them all over the dining room.
*Then, the kids made a graph of how many "A" words, "B" words, etc.
*We left these words up for a couple of weeks because the kids kept thinking of more math words to add.
*Each person chose a famous mathematician and wrote a short paragraph about him and shared it with everyone.
*We played several math games (There are many good ideas in *Family Math* by Jean Kerr Stenmark)
*We worked on their regular math work, for example:
>   *Math in careers
>   *Math in the kitchen
>   *Math history
>   *Writing checks
>   *Having a pretend business
>   *Doing math riddles

We also did a **Power History Day** and these are some of the things we did:
>   *Read about American Indians
>   *Learned some Cherokee language
>   *We made an Indian food called pemmican
>   *We made leather crafts
>   *We wrote reports

    *We played authentic games

Here are some other ideas for Power Days:

Power Music Day
*History of music
*Composers
*Listen to great music
*Peter and the Wolf
*Music games (name that tune or count that measure)
*Music theory
*Talk about different instruments
*Writing music
*Singing

Power Geography Day
*Label as much as you can on a blank map
*Continents
*Countries
*Read road maps, plan family vacation route
*Traditions
*Flags
*Differences
*Languages
*Make your favorite flag
*Geography games

Power Science Day
*Fun experiments that teach specific principles
*Maybe stick with 1 to 5 principles the entire day, depending on complexity.
*Graph and chart results
*Kitchen science
*National Geographic Videos (We enjoyed one recently about horseshoe crabs.)
*Study anatomy, put a skeleton together and name major bones
*Learn about the eyeball and label its parts

131

The Big GIANT Decision...Homeschool!   By Penni Renee Pierce

Power Days can be really fun! We only had two the whole year, because they take a lot of preparation. But, once we had one, the kids begged for another Power Day! They are really great and the children look forward to them.

Chapter 13
INTERVIEWS
One-on-one Meeting With Your Children

When we started homeschool, I decided to interview the children three times per year. This would be a one-on-one meeting with no distractions. This was done at the beginning of the year, right after Christmas and then right before the end of the year. These are the questions I asked first after we had done homeschool for only two weeks:

*What do you like most about homeschool?
*Of which subjects would you like to study more? How are
  you going to accomplish this?
*Of all the subjects we've been doing, which one do
  you think you need to spend more time?

As I interviewed them, I wrote down their answers and helped them set goals. At our next interview, I basically asked the same questions and reviewed their former interview answers with them.

My final interview went something like this:

  "We've had a wonderful year; we've done many
  things."
*Do you feel good about the year?
*Is there anything you would like to change for next
  year?
 *What would you like to accomplish this summer?

I always try to find positive things to say to each one of them about their progress! Interviews are fun and there is a close feeling between my children and myself at this time. It is also refreshing to hear their opinion and get to know them better. I strongly recommend doing this with your children whether you do homeschool or not. Dad could also do interviews to help children set goals.

By interviewing your children, you will be able to stay on top of things. Interviews will also help them to set goals and see their own progress.

NOTE: I still do these interviews with Briana and Kyla especially right before we start a new year.

A TV interviewer once asked American school children how they could make higher grades in math. The children answered that they could not do better, "I'm just not smart in math", was the common reply. When Asian school children were asked the same question, they answered something like this: "If I put forth the effort, I can accomplish anything." Wow, what a difference in attitudes.

134

The Big GIANT Decision...Homeschool! By Penni Renee Pierce

Chapter 14
HOW TO HAVE A HOMESCHOOL OPEN HOUSE
Get Ready, Set Up, Go!

The Idea

In the *Home School Manual* by Theodore E. Wade there is the idea of a homeschool Open House. I was so excited about doing this! We are very blessed to have grandparents, aunts, uncles and cousins close enough to come. If you don't have many relatives nearby, then think about maybe inviting soccer coaches, dance teachers, Sunday school teachers, bishops, pastors or close friends.

Get Ready

I wanted to do this because I felt it would be fun for the kids to display their work for the year. Also, they could give a short recital at this time. So, we started planning. Right away, the kids picked which songs they would play at Open House. Their music practicing picked up immediately. They had something special to work toward. I had been saving all the papers they had done the entire year anyway. So I just needed to gather things up and keep them in an Open House File. When it came close to our Open House date, we designed, on a computer, the invitations and programs. Thanks to my father-in-law; he has a wonderful computer and color printer. We started deciding how to rearrange the furniture in the house to accommodate all the displays and about 40 people. We took all the furniture out of our dining room and living room. We had about eight display tables. We borrowed tables from family and friends. We covered every table with white tablecloths that hung to the floor. This was great because we could store any excess school supplies under these tables after we had set up.

Set Up

We decided to have a History Table, Science Table, Math Table, Religion Table, Creative Writing Table, Notes from the Teacher Table, Reading Table, Art Wall, Summer Fun Display, and an Under Construction Display and even a small display of our preschoolers' work.

We designed, on the computer, a sign for each table with colored pictures. For example, for the History Table, we had a picture of George Washington and for the Religion Table, we had a picture of Christ. We mounted these pictures and signs on colored paper.

Also, I stapled the children's work onto colored paper. This made everything look new and fresh.

On our History Table we had leather work, authentic paper dolls from the Colonial era, history reports, books we read, American flags, replica money from the 1800's and our Declaration of Independence papers (as explained in the History chapter of this book).

On our Science Table we had science books, Tahnee's monkey report, rock, diamond and volcano reports and an entire rock collection, labeled.

On our Math Table, we had our math books displayed, fraction bars, Number Jumbler, triangle flashcards and workbooks.

On our Religion Table we displayed beautiful pictures of the Savior from birth to crucifixion and our scriptures and the kids' posters of scripture stories.

On the Creative Writing Table we had stories of historical events from an animal's point of view, fractured fairy tales, and all the language books we used.

On the Notes from the Teacher Table, I wrote a little note saying how I have enjoyed our first year of homeschool and some of our experiences.

On the Reading Table, each child had an area to display their books they have read for the entire year. This was one of our largest displays.

On the Art Wall, were displayed, on colored paper, many drawings the kids had done throughout the year. They happen to be very artistic, so there were many drawings we could not put up. But, we had an entire wall covered and a sign that said, "Artists at Work".

Our Summer Fun Display was on top of a bookshelf. I displayed things we had purchased to do for the summer, such as science experiments and art history.

On our Under Construction Table we put all the fabric and notions we had purchased to make our Homeschool banner. We could not finish it in time for Open House, so my mom suggested that we display it with an "Under Construction" sign on it. It is going to be beautiful. The kids helped choose their school colors, which are turquoise and silver. Since we are part Cherokee they felt these colors would represent the American Indian part of our heritage. The banner will say M.D. Pierce Academy, named after the man who funds our private school, my husband. On the bottom of our banner, it will say, in the Cherokee language, "Seekers of Good Books"- "O sda di go we la tsu yo hi".

We also put up some drawings our little preschoolers had done throughout the year and displayed some games they like to play, such as "Playful Patterns" by Discovery Toys. We also had them put their hands in different colored paint and put prints on white paper. Then, we cut out each little hand and made "hand chains" by stapling the hands together. It looked adorable for their little display.

Also, we displayed, throughout the house, books we had used the whole year. There were about 86 books. There would have been more, but we can only check out a limited number from the library. I kept an ongoing list of library books we had enjoyed during the year. So, when we were preparing for Open House, I checked out as many as we could for our display. Every book anyone saw at Open House, we had either read it aloud, read it individually or used it as a reference.

136

The Big GIANT Decision...Homeschool!   By Penni Renee Pierce

We also had pictures of the kids on different field trips throughout the year, recess and pictures of daily school activities. These were placed in a large collage with captions.

Accomplishments

As we gathered up all of the materials for Open House, the kids could not believe all the things we had accomplished for the year. They were impressed with the display of all the books they had read. The children did not realize all they had done until they saw all of the materials out at the same time.

That Night...

We had our Open House from 7 until 8 PM. We all dressed up for this. I gave a little speech about the kids before their recital. The kids' performance was only 10 minutes long, so everyone had plenty of time to see the displays and leave when they wanted. We served sugar cookies, strawberries and dip and a clear punch. It was a very successful and special event!

EXTRA NOTE: Our homeschool open house is one of our special memories. I have not had another open house since that first year.

The reward of a thing well done, is to have done it.
-Ralph Waldo Emerson

137

The Big GIANT Decision...Homeschool!   By Penni Renee Pierce

Chapter 15
GETTING ORGANIZED
Chaos, Supplies, Chores, etc.

Chaos

One person's definition of the word "organization" might be another person's definition of "chaos". I believe in being organized. But, organizing your life does not happen over night.

Homeschool Stuff

The first thing I did after returning from my first homeschool book fair was to get a large binder (3-ring notebook). There were tons of information at the book fair, so I placed dividers in my notebook and labeled the dividers according to the company handouts and catalogs that I had received. This paid off later as a real time saver. Many times while referring back to this material, it was easy to find the divider and get what was needed. Once I even had to refer back to some information for a lady I met at the park. She had many questions about homeschool and it felt good to be able to get my hands on the information and help her.

School Supplies

In our living room, we have baskets that stack on top of one another. Each one is labeled "Math", "Science", "Language", etc. We put all our materials, we are using, at the time, in these baskets. When the kids are finished with math, all their materials go back in the "Math" basket. This keeps things from being lost under beds and behind bookshelves! We also have a cabinet where we keep all of our pens, pencils, glue, markers, colored paper, stapler, tape, etc.

Opportunity is missed by most people because it comes dressed in overalls and looks like work.

-Thomas Edison

Chores

Another thing about having order in your home will involve training your children with some weekly cleaning jobs. We had trained our children to do these chores long before we started homeschool. We taught them how to vacuum and sweep; how to clean a bathroom; how to clean the kitchen; how to dust and how to make their beds and organize their rooms. This was not an easy task to do, but once they learned it, they could really serve their family and make a contribution. Teaching involves showing them many times until they understand what is expected. If you have not yet

138

The Big GIANT Decision...Homeschool!   By Penni Renee Pierce

taught your child a family cleaning job, do not announce you are going to do homeschool and teach how to clean the bathroom in the same breath. They may think that homeschool means, I have to do chores. NOT SO; children should have family responsibilities no matter what school they attend! Assign chores in the summer, then start your homeschool in the fall. That way, you will have time to establish your routine and chores will not be associated with homeschool.

Rotate

Our children do their chores twice weekly and then rotate. For instance, the vacuum person for that week vacuums Monday and Friday and then it rotates to the next person the following Monday. They also rotate cleaning the kitchen every evening.

Yours, Mine and Ours

I clean my room and bathroom. I cook all the meals unless they want to and I keep the kitchen clean throughout the day. I do most of the laundry. Sometimes, I have them help sort. We also purchased, for our laundry, the same type baskets that we purchased for our school materials. Everyone has their own basket and as soon as the clothes come out of the dryer, they go into the correct basket. Then everyone is responsible for putting their things away (At least that is how it should happen; some people have to be reminded).

Be Happy!

If you have tiny children and you are homeschooling, of course you will be the "sole" housecleaner for a while. But, your children will soon grow and learn their responsibilities.

Keeping your daily routine and house cleaning chores done and delegated will make life happier and help your homeschooling experiences be more fun!

EXTRA NOTE: Briana and Kyla are 15 and 13 now. They have two dish chores per week. They clean the upstairs bathroom two times per week. They sweep and dust the upstairs hall and the stairs. They feed, walk and bathe their shih-tzu puppies. They feed the cats and help clean when we have company. They do laundry. They gather eggs and help in the garden. I once had a mother tell me that her 17-year-old daughter did not do any chores and that she didn't even have her daughter make her own bed because her daughter just had too many extra curricular activities which made it impossible for her to help around the house!!! I hope that young lady learns how to wash a dish and clean a house before she leaves home!! I wouldn't want her for a college roommate, that's for sure!!!! When children do not help around the house they become detached from the family and selfish.

140

The Big GIANT Decision...Homeschool! By Penni Renee Pierce

Chapter 16
FIRED UP AND BURNED OUT
What on earth did I get myself into?

Where's The Matches?

It makes one wonder why they call it that; "burned out"?! Imagine a candle burning until it uses up every bit of wax. We can replace the candle easily, but it just takes some of us longer to find the matches!

What On Earth Did I Get Myself Into?

There is nothing uncommon about losing the initial enthusiasm for a project; whether it be starting college, taking a new class, building a piece of furniture, etc. You gather up all your materials and prepare for your new project. But, as time goes on (as we know time does), we lose our energy, we question our decision, we think, "What on earth did I get myself into?". When this happens, if we go back and look at the reasons for our decisions, what motivated us in the first place and ask how did we feel in our hearts at the start, then we will remember our purpose.

A Break!

The day after day routine of math, language, history and being with the children 24 hours a day may make you feel the need for a little break. You might just need to change your schedule. You may need to have an arts and crafts day. You also may need to go on a field trip or just take a day off. There is nothing wrong with that! You may need to go for a long walk by yourself!

Am I Doing Enough?

Homeschooling parents are always checking and re-checking themselves to make sure they are doing enough. In talking with other parents I see that they have this stress, which I have felt also. In most cases, homeschool parents are doing a wonderful job and are doing plenty for and with their children.

No School

Once, late at night, I knew I needed a break. So, I made a sign that said, "NO SCHOOL. ARTS AND CRAFTS DAY" and put it on the dining room table. The kids were very excited when they woke up the next morning and saw the sign. We spent the day painting and making decorations for the holidays.

141

The Big GIANT Decision...Homeschool! By Penni Renee Pierce

Reading Day

Some homeschooling families have a reading day and they read the entire day. The children read their own books and/or the mother reads aloud to them.

4-Day Weekend

I remember once, we took two days off right before a weekend in order to have four straight days to play and goof off. We did not do anything special. But, everyone felt very refreshed by Monday.

Books, Book Fairs, People

Sometimes parents need to be fired up. We need to find the matches. Reading a homeschooling book or going to the next homeschooling book fair can help. It can be inspiring to look at all the materials available to homeschoolers. You may want to talk to a friend that homeschools, also. Talking to others in the same situation helps tremendously. Many cities have homeschool co-ops and support groups. Homeschool has become so widespread that finding out about co-ops or support groups should be fairly easy. Ask people at church or school if they know anyone that homeschools. Once you find one homeschooling family, you will find many. Also, in Donn Reed's *The Home School Source Book,* there is listed under "Support Groups" the homeschool groups in each state and Canada.

EXTRA Note: Also, if you go to www.hslda.org and click "support groups", you will find all the support groups in your state.

Organize and Exercise

Sometimes, just organizing your house and straightening things will help your outlook. Exercising and eating right will definitely give you a better attitude.

Are You Convinced?

Burnout, whether short-term or long-term, is common for everyone. The key is to be very convinced of the reasons you are doing homeschool before you ever start. If those reasons are strong and real, then you will be able to overcome a lack of enthusiasm every once in a while.

Variety

Sometimes, just adding something new to your curricula will add variety. We recently added music and art appreciation. It is fun and different from our routine.

142

The Big GIANT Decision...Homeschool! By Penni Renee Pierce

Find The Matches!

Homeschooling your children is a big, gigantic responsibility. You can be sure that there will be a lack of enthusiasm either on your part or your children. But, also along with this big, gigantic responsibility come days that you will never forget, days <u>they</u> will never forget, times where you laugh joyfully with your children, times when you cry during history, scripture names and places no one can pronounce, a piano piece finally perfected, an unsolicited oral book report by your 13-year-old, a great quantity of time spent with your children and the list goes on and on and on.

Expect burnout. It happens. Learn to find the matches if it does. Give yourself the time. The children will be fine, even if you're having a bad day (week).

Chapter 17
A FATHER'S THOUGHTS ON HOMESCHOOL
"One day my wife called me at work…"

One day my wife called me at work and said, "I'm supposed to do homeschool!" This was a surprise to me. Our past thoughts on homeschooling were that it was only done by those that were extreme or maybe even fanatical. When we relocated to Richardson, my wife and I became acquainted with a family that we respected and admired and who happened to be homeschooling their children. Through this family we were re-introduced to homeschooling. We later found out that many people, we knew before we were married, were homeschooling their children.

I supported my wife with homeschooling and knew that she felt inspired to do this, however I still had the typical concerns, such as; Would they learn what they need to know?, Would they stick to a schedule?, Would losing contact with other children be harmful?

When they started, I immediately noticed several things. The children were less stressed. They started enjoying learning. They started to enjoy reading books. They became happier children. I saw them getting up and starting their school work on their own.

My concerns went away. I saw my children learn faster and better. I saw them not stressed about learning and therefore enjoying learning and reading. My concern about their "losing out" on socialization went away. They have friends at church, other homeschool children, cousins and our own family. I think that one of the most important things my children have learned is that they can learn on their own and they do not have to be spoon-fed knowledge. They have taught themselves to play the piano and to play the guitar, with our help on theory and technique.

My wife is doing a tremendous job. She has accomplished things and uncovered talents and abilities she would have never known or used unless she had done homeschool. Our children are benefiting greatly from this creative and unhindered way of learning and my wife is right beside them enjoying and learning, too. I am in total support.

Mark Pierce

EXTRA NOTE: Another benefit of homeschooling is that we gained control of our time instead of being subject to homework, cramming for tests, staying up late doing book reports, etc. When we started homeschooling we had more time and we could decide whenever we wanted to take days off and we enjoyed the benefit of vacationing in the off seasons.   -Mark

144

The Big GIANT Decision...Homeschool! By Penni Renee Pierce

Chapter 18
THE HOMESCHOOL GRADUATE GOES TO COLLEGE
Kindergarten, First Grade...College! That Fast!
Sample High School Transcript

About Our Graduates

We now have three graduated homeschoolers. Mark would like to be an engineer. He is very talented in physics and math, as I stated before. Rachel will be a registered nurse in about four months. She is the one who, during homeschool, would practically climb under the table if I even mentioned the word "vein". Everything about biology made her skin crawl. I am proud to say that Rachel has "almost" fainted only two times while giving an IV to a patient! However, she is doing much better now. Tahnee was our child that made up her own sounds and words for things starting at about age 5. We always would say, "Tahnee speaks another language". Just teasing, of course. As she became older she studied French through the Power-Glide program and we realized she had an incredible talent for picking up foreign languages. She loves French, but has also taken Spanish, Russian and some Latin. Mark, Rachel and Tahnee have always had to work hard in school for their grades. It really paid off because at the end of many of their college semesters, they were straight "A" students. Rachel and Tahnee both received academic scholarships. I guess what I am trying to say is that homeschooling works. Our kids did well in spite of any weaknesses I felt I had in any given subject.

Lessons Learned

Next, I would like to share with you some things that we learned about transitioning from homeschool to college, our experiences getting our kids into the local community colleges and why they chose to go locally first.

"Cream of the Crop"

Many colleges are now assigning a staff member to be their Homeschool Coordinators. The Homeschool Coordinator specifically helps the incoming homeschool high school graduates. One Homeschooling Coordinator said to me that the homeschoolers are the "cream of the crop"! I thought that was an interesting observation. I feel that homeschoolers become self-motivated learners and develop such excellent study habits in the home that college is a very smooth transition for them. Here is a list of things you need to think about to prepare your child for college:

1) **HIGH SCHOOL SUBJECT REQUIREMENTS**: Find out from the public school district in your area what subjects are required for a student to graduate from high school.

2) **PLANNED COURSE OF STUDY**: Make sure that you focus on these subjects starting at age 13 to 14. Have a planned course of study.

3) **COMMUNITY COLLEGE REQUIREMENTS**: Find out from your community college what they require for a homeschooler to enter their college. (If you call while your child is 14, make sure you call again right before they enter, because requirements are changing quite often.)

4) **UNIVERSITY REQUIREMENTS**: If your child wants to go directly to a University, then you need to find out about the homeschool requirements for that University and your child will probably need to take the ACT or SAT. So, you may want to start doing practice testing for those tests.

5) **THE TRANSCRIPT**: Put together your homeschool transcript. Remember this is based on your research of your State Laws for homeschooling and your knowledge of what a graduating senior is required to take in high school.

I would like to elaborate about each of the five things listed above.

1) High School Subject Requirements: How did I find out what the required high school subjects were? I had a friend who had kids in high school and she told me the required subjects for the high school near us. She was very involved in her children's education and I trusted her. You can also easily find this information on the internet or your nearest school district office. This is very helpful information and gives your course of study direction.

2) Planned Course of Study: As you are made aware of subject requirements for your area, you will be prepared to make a plan. We have done this as we went along while I researched curricula. I have chosen things along the way that have fit into this plan. Or, many homeschoolers buy complete materials, for example, everything you need for 10th grade in one package. I have friends that enter their children in a distance learning private school starting in the ninth grade and then the child later becomes a high school graduate from that school.

3) Community College Requirements: As you check with your local community colleges about their requirements for homeschoolers, it will give you an idea of what you need to be doing. Check with several. I had a "run in" with a counselor at a community college who wanted me to submit a detailed description of all courses my child had taken. So, I proceeded home and began to type up every concept they had ever learned in Saxon math. That, in itself, would have been a 30 page document! Then if you included all the other things we had done in homeschool for their high school years, I could have submitted a 100 page document. The "evil" side of me really wanted to do this and

146

The Big GIANT Decision...Homeschool!   By Penni Renee Pierce

drop the heavy document onto his "self-important" desk! Instead, I headed for a different office and talked to a different person who was a little more educated about homeschool! Your child will need a high school transcript and some sort of ID to register at a community college. Then, he will schedule a time to go and take the placement test for that college. The placement test is a test to place your student in the correct math and language courses at their college. We chose community college first because our kids were finished with homeschool at about age 16 and were ready to attend college, which they did. Community college is also cheaper for the general education requirements for one thing and I felt it was a good place for our kids to start and get the feel of college. If you know which university your student would like to attend, then work closely with that university and also the community college (if they will be a transfer student entering the university) you have chosen; making sure that the classes transfer. I think the *inability* to transfer classes from one college to the other is the biggest scam in the college system. I think that all colleges and universities are guilty of it. The fact that when you transfer to a university and have to take the same, exact course of study over because the university will not accept it from the community college is an insult to the student and to the college. So, pay close attention and remember that requirements for transfer credits could change on any given year. Some community colleges have started honors high school classes that homeschoolers can take also. All of our homeschool graduates, so far have entered universities as "transfer students" from our local community colleges. We had no problem with this. Now, I have found that some of the requirements about transfer students have changed, so make sure you comply and check with the university. I think the universities are trying to stop "young" (meaning 16 & 17 year olds) from attending. Instead, the student is having to wait until they are considered "graduation" age, which is 17 or 18. Also, the student will be required by the university to have a certain amount of community college credits to enter that university as a "transfer student". For example, a university may require that a student have 30 community college credit hours and 28 of those must be from core curricula, meaning general education. The university can give you a list of what their core curricula requirements are. Make sure the core curriculum courses your student takes at community college will transfer to the university they have chosen, as I stated above. Sometimes the university may require the student to email or fax the university a copy of the course description to see if it matches the university's requirements for that particular course.

4) University Requirements: If your child is a transfer student from a community college and they have good grades, he may not be required to take the SAT or ACT. Find out, so that you don't waste time taking that test. However, if your child goes *directly* from homeschool to a university, then it is almost certain he or she will need to take one of these tests. There are internet sites where your children can practice taking the tests and also you can go to your public library and get books about how to take the SAT or ACT.

5) *The Transcript:* As I stated above, you need to know the requirements for graduation from high school in your area and focus your plan of study on that. Here is a sample transcript. Keep in mind, in the state of Texas, if you homeschool, your homeschool is considered a *private school*. I also have our kids' transcripts notarized. I probably do not need to have this extra feature, but I feel it is a further witness that we, as parents did in deed sign this document and verify that he/she graduated from high school. All states are different about this. So, it will require your own research. We do not give grades or grade point average in our homeschool. The student just completes and passes the course of study. Your area may require grades!

SAMPLE TRANSCRIPT

M.D. Pierce Academy
A private homeschool

TRANSCRIPT FOR

DOB: ADDRESS:

PHONE:

(Graduation Date:)

CURRICULUM	CREDITS	COURSES
Mathematics	3	General Math
		Geometry
		Algebra
English	4	English I, II, III & IV
Social Studies	4	United States History
		Ancient World History
		Geography
		US Government/Economics
Foreign Language	3	French I & II
		Latin I
Science	3	Biology/Anatomy
		Physical Science/Earth Science
		Health
Fine Arts	1	Art History
Computer	1	Word Processing
Physical Education	2	Soccer .5
		Irish Dance .5
		Running .5
		Weights .5
Theology	4	Completed four years of early morning seminary
		(scripture study course)
TOTAL CREDITS	25	

M.D. Pierce Academy hereby announces that (Name of Student) has completed her High School Requirements in a bona fide manner in the state of Texas, being an excellent, self-motivated learner. As of , (Date) he/she is a graduated senior from M.D. Pierce Academy (A private homeschool) in Texas.

_____
Mother
_____*DATE*

_____
Father
_____*DATE*

_____*Notary*   _____*DATE*

Chapter 19
GRADUATED HOMESCHOOLERS' COMMENTARY
Graduates Give Thoughts, Advice And Experiences About Homeschool

Mark's Homeschool Memories & Transitioning Into College

One thing that comes to mind was reading *Johnny Tremain*. Mom read it aloud to us. It was a very good story. I probably liked our study of the Bible the most. The Old Testament was very interesting. When I was a kid I felt that school was school, you had to do it. I did not like Math, at all. I enjoy Math now. I enjoyed learning about the Acadians and reading the poem "Evangeline" with another homeschooling family.

When I was a kid I realized I had to finish my school work, so I just did it. Now that I am in college, I realize the benefit of having learned how to study on my own, because that is required in college. As a homeschooler, you learn to become self-motivated which really helps you in college.

In doing homeschool, my hours were much more flexible to have a job. I started my own lawn mowing business at age 13. I learned how to be a self-directed worker. I was able to earn enough money to buy a very expensive guitar. Also, we had plenty of time to have our own band and practice whenever we needed.

I took a computer programming class when I first went to college. I was 16 years old. I think I felt nervous when I first went to college, I don't remember. But, I do remember that I understood the class material.

When I came back from my mission, I took a college level Algebra class. I hardly had to study. I just made A's because I had really learned math well in homeschool.

There was no gap for me in the transition from homeschool to college. All of the college material was easy for me to understand. We did not do Chemistry in homeschool, so I didn't feel very prepared for college Chemistry, however I studied hard and made a B in Chemistry I and I am currently making an A in Chemistry II.

Rachel's Homeschool Memories & Transitioning Into College

There are many homeschool activities that stand out in my mind the most. I really enjoyed studying Egypt and making a relief map of Egypt out of clay. We studied rocks and minerals and then went to a Rock and Mineral Show. We were able to identify rocks that we had studied. After that we went to the Diamond Mines in Arkansas. That was really fun! I loved to play piano for an hour or so a day. I did this whenever I wanted. We studied the Acadians and read the poem "Evangeline". It was very interesting. I loved working on the science experiments and Tahnee and I made a science kit and our granddad and grandmother gave us some science equipment. We had the opportunity

150

The Big GIANT Decision...Homeschool! By Penni Renee Pierce

to have a band. We were able to practice whenever we wanted. We performed at our church youth conference a couple of times. Homeschool afforded us the opportunity to work on music arrangements during the school day. I enjoyed our Homeschool Choir too! We were able to sing and perform. We sang "In The Jungle" and some other fun choir arrangements and I also provided the piano accompaniment for the choir sometimes. We studied about Colonial days, what they wore and how they lived. I loved studying out of a medical book from the olden days. Mom read this aloud to us. It was a crazy book with funny things they used to do, for example in order to help your cold or illness, you were to put two eels in a bowl by your bed to help you get well. This is funny to me, especially now that I am in nursing school! I loved studying about ancient Greece, Rome and Egypt. I especially enjoyed Greece and would love to travel there one day!

I liked the fact that my Mom helped us learn to love learning. And we didn't have dates and dead lines. Learning is not a "one time" event, it is a continuous part of life.

I felt nervous about going to college, but I felt I was ready to go. I feel that I was at an age to go, ready to get out of the house. I wasn't nervous about the classes. I felt like I could do the work. I did not feel it was too high of a step for me. I felt like I already knew how to study, because at home you are studying by yourself much of the time and we understood that we were responsible for our own education, not Mom in particularly. I did not know what I wanted to study in college, so I took many different classes.   The transition from homeschool to college was easy and it helped too that I had homeschooling friends going into college at the same time.   Which also made the transition very fun!

Tahnee's Homeschooling Memories & Transitioning Into College

My favorite thing about homeschool is learning. I love to learn any subject! But, I have to say my favorites were subjects that dealt with people, their culture and life style, for example American History, World History and Foreign Languages. Come to think of it, I liked every subject including Science, Music, Literature, Scripture Study; every subject except for MATH. I really despise Math. I am sorry if that offends anyone! But, the truth is fact! I really enjoyed Power Days. That is when we would study a subject for the entire day or week, such as American Indians and Pilgrims. We did arts & crafts and we made food from the time period. I was very intrigued and remembered it!

One thing that excited me the most about homeschool was the fact that you do not need a teacher for every subject. Because I discovered that you can learn about anything by researching it yourself. I had started two big research projects myself because I wanted to learn about Cowboys and the western frontier. I checked out books from the library and did a huge research paper about it. Also, I wanted to learn about the United States. I had a notebook and each week I learned about one state and I would put the research in the notebook, i.e. history, facts, population, industry, state bird, etc. I did all of this because I wanted to. Mom did not assign it!

I would read a lot of biographies about anyone I wanted to learn about in history. I loved learning Greek, Roman and Egyptian History!

The transition from homeschool to college was scary, but I think any graduate from any public or private school will experience the same feelings. Nevertheless, I was very eager and ready to go to college. There was no hesitation. I was excited, but still a little nervous! I was 16 when I took my first community college assessment test. I did very well. The first college class I walked into was French. Many of the people in the class had taken French in high school and thankfully I had studied some French in the Power-Glide program which prepared me for a college class. At first, I was uncertain about how hard the class was going to be, but soon realized that it wasn't bad at all. I just had to do the work and I really enjoyed it. As a matter of fact, French has become my favorite foreign language.

On Preparing For College- Advice On Course Of Study

On the *sample transcript* above, you will see the subjects that we studied in homeschool. Also, there are some subjects that my homeschool graduates suggested that I do with Briana and Kyla *in addition* to these. So, I listed below the subjects that Mark, Rachel and Tahnee feel would be helpful to any homeschooler before entering college. The first one is Biology. I did an introduction to Biology with the kids, but Tahnee said that most of the people in her college Biology class had already had Biology in high school. She said that the subject seemed entirely new to her. Besides just an introduction to Biology, she wished she had studied at least **Biology I** also before entering college. However, she did say that she studied very hard and made an "A" in the college course. Mark suggested a focus on **Reading Comprehension**. Since, all assessment tests for community college have Reading Comprehension, this would be very helpful. Rachel suggests doing **Dictation** with your children. We did do dictation in our homeschool. She said this really helped her in learning to take notes in college. You really do not have to buy a structured course for this. You can just dictate excerpts from scripture or classic novels and have your children write what you speak. Also, I suggest that in addition to doing General Math, Pre-algebra & Algebra I, that you also complete the entire course of **Algebra II** before entering college. This will enable your student to take the math portion of the assessment test for community college and do well. If they score low on that portion of the math section, they will have to take a remedial math class. The remedial class in college will cost money and time and they will not get college credit for it.

If they *do* have to take remedial math or remedial language classes in college, the benefit is that those remedial classes will prepare them to then take the college math and college language courses. It is just better and cheaper to get all of the required math and language finished before they start college.

NOTE: The next chapter contains a poem. It is entitled *Every Child's Dream*. I wrote it in 1990. It was inspired by my husband and his mother when Mark would reminisce about growing up. I wanted to add this to the book because it says so much about motherhood and I feel that mothers have such a profound impact on the future of our world. This is dedicated to my husband Mark and his mother, Leda who was always there for him.

153

The Big GIANT Decision...Homeschool!   By Penni Renee Pierce

Chapter 20

EVERY CHILD'S DREAM   by Penni Renee Pierce

"Hey Mom, I'm home", were the first words from his mouth.
As he eagerly pushes the door to get inside.

His dusty blonde hair,
Wind blown and free
Swept across his face.

He walks the path of the well-worn carpet
that leads directly to the kitchen;

His lips smiling at the smell of cinnamon
And fresh apples.

He sees the face of his mother,
As she tossels his hair and squeezes his chin.

He watches her as she makes the recipe,
Tenderly measuring each ingredient,
As if each were more precious than the one before.

He grabs a tall glass from the cupboard
And pours himself some cold milk.

He hops upon the kitchen counter
to peek inside the cookie jar,
Almost holding his breath to see the surprise!

He snatches three large oatmeal cookies
And skips over to the table;
The taste feels so good in his mouth
And his mother asks about his day.

When years are swept away,
He tenderly remembers the comfortable home,
The security
And love.
And only when he is grown
With a family of his own,
Do the words echo through his mind...
"Hey Mom, I'm home".
And she was.

It's every child's dream.

154

The Big GIANT Decision...Homeschool! By Penni Renee Pierce

Chapter 21
THE HOMESCHOOL GUARANTEE
It's Not A Piece of Cake- It Is A Celebration!

Homeschooling is hard work.
You have to plan and organize.
You can't go shopping or play tennis or jazzercise or have your hair done while the kids are at school, because
school is you.
You have to be there for them.
You have to reorganize your life.
You have to want this experience for them.
You have to realize and know that what you are doing is right for your family.
You need the support of your spouse.
If you're quitting work to do this, you need to understand that you will be doing without some material items.
There are good days in homeschooling.
There are not-so-good days.
You have to spend a little money here and there.
Not all at once, if you can't, but here and there.
It's not a piece of cake.
It is a celebration.
You will grow with your children.
You will open up communication with your children you have never had before.
You will become excited about the materials available.
You will dream of fun things and ways to help them learn.
Your family will realize unity.
The memories will be endless.
Your children will experience freedom; the
FREEDOM TO LEARN!

by Penni Renee' Pierce

Men occasionally stumble over the truth, but most of them pick themselves up and hurry off as if nothing has happened.

-Sir Winston Churchill

The Big GIANT Decision...Homeschool! By Penni Renee Pierce

155

LAST EXTRA NOTE: Many of the ideas in this book are not new because all who profess that homeschool is wonderful and worthwhile are "standing on the shoulders of the giants" who pioneered it. I realize that. I built my conclusions, ideas, techniques and enthusiasm from reading many, many books, catalogs, websites, prayer and from talking to homeschooling parents for the last 13 years. So many people, whom I have never met, have done so much to make homeschooling a reality. Our family has reaped the rewards of an incredible educational experience!

Education is the key to unlock the golden door of freedom.
-George Washington Carver

Best Wishes!
-Penni Pierce

156

The Big GIANT Decision...Homeschool! By Penni Renee Pierce

ACKNOWLEDGMENTS
I could not have done it without you...

Thank you to my husband, who was always very supportive. And my children for being my inspiration for the first edition and writing their thoughts for the second edition. Without them, there would have been no homeschool experience at all!

I sincerely appreciate my father and mother-in-law, Charles and Leda Pierce for letting me spend many hours on their computer writing the first edition of this book. They always made me feel comfortable and welcome and kept the kids occupied while I typed. Also, I thank them for taking their time to help edit and add some wonderful ideas. And a BIG special thank you to Dad Pierce for spending a tremendous amount of time with me doing the book layout.

I thank my mother, Michelle Scott-Chiodo for helping with editing. Thanks Mom!

Thanks to my sister and brother-in-law, Milley and Pekka Aalto for scanning photographs for the first edition of the book and being so willing to help out.

I'm thankful for Pearl and Andy Anderson who took time to read and discuss a very rough draft of the first edition. My thanks to Andy for the wonderful Foreword. Pearl and Andy have passed away since the writing of the first edition and I express my sincere love and appreciation to their large family!

I appreciate my friend Christie Atkinson and the time she has spent with me, answering my questions and giving book recommendations. Her enthusiasm is addictive and encouraging!

Also, thanks to Wendy Hansen, for taking time to give book recommendations.

As I have worked on the second edition, my sister Terri has given me lots of encouragement, "Hurry up and finish the book, there are people who want it!" and her wonderful ideas and experience teaching music in the public schools.

My little brother is the best, he is twenty years younger than I am and was born into the technological era. I have had to ask tons of questions that he answered and he has been so patient with his computer challenged sister! Thanks little, tiny brother!!!! Also, his wife Amy teaches voice, piano and acting. She helped me so much with the Music section of the Resource Guide. Thanks so much!

-Penni

YEARBOOK

M.D. PIERCE ACADEMY

Our First Year

*1994 Back: Rachel, Mark, Tahnee
Stroller: Briana & Kyla*

*Tahnee, Mark, Rachel
"Brotherly Love"*

HOMESCHOOL YEARBOOK

Our Little Kyla Rose
1 Year Old

We start homeschool early at our house!

Dad & Briana

FAMILY   HOME   LOVE

HOMESCHOOL YEARBOOK

They are not supposed to pull the cushions off!

Kyla 1, Rachel 11, Tahnee 9, Briana 2
Our First Year of Homeschool

FAMILY FUN!!

HOMESCHOOL YEARBOOK

Rachel learning the flute. However piano became her favorite! Age 11

MUSIC

Mark practicing the guitar. Age 13
He mowed a lot of lawns for this guitar!

Tahnee practicing piano. Age 9

Notes   Measures   Beats

HOMESCHOOL YEARBOOK

Briana & Rachel cutting out pictures
And making what I like to call a "Happy Mess"!

Tahnee age 9 & Kyla age 1
Being very Patriotic!!

"And the home of the brave..."

HOMESCHOOL YEARBOOK

Stephen Atkinson, Jamie Atkinson, Rachel Pierce, Leah Atkinson,
Dwain Atkinson, Tahnee Pierce, Mark Pierce & David Chiodo
Pig Sty!!!
Farmstead, Plano, Texas 1994

Tahnee and Mark working in the dining room on homeschool.
A rare moment when they are not annoying each other!

Pigs   Cows   Chickens   Exponent   Ratio

HOMESCHOOL YEARBOOK

Mark and Mom working on Math. This has to be a posed picture.
Mark doesn't smile that much while doing Math!

Math　　Science　　Language　　Home

Briana
Our Little Sweetheart!

HOMESCHOOL YEARBOOK

Kyla & Briana doing a News & Weather Report
Ages 8 & 9

"Looks like there are some clouds moving in from the west,
but only a 10% chance of showers. Back to you Kyla!"

HOMESCHOOL YEARBOOK

Briana & Kyla working on school at our new,
100 year old farm house.

Briana working on school in the car!

Kids At Work!

While Mom & Dad scrape, sand and paint
Kyla finishes her math.

HOMESCHOOL YEARBOOK

Seniors

Mark Daniel Pierce
Homeschool Graduate
Age 16

Rachel Michelle Pierce
Homeschool Graduate
Age 16

HOMESCHOOL YEARBOOK

Seniors

Tahnee Renee Pierce
Homeschool Graduate
Age 16

Hip Hip Hooray!

HOMESCHOOL YEARBOOK

Marriage *Love* *Forever*

Mark & Christy Pierce
Married June 3, 2005

Rachel & Eric Allphin
Married August 6, 2005

The Beginning

HOMESCHOOL YEARBOOK

Hope　　Future　　Life　　Fun　　Joy

Tahnee Renee Pierce

20 years old

Linguistics Major

She would like to be an Interpreter and teach

English as a second language.

HOMESCHOOL YEARBOOK

Dance   Art   Sing   Dance   Art   Sing

Briana Veronika Pierce

She is 14 years old here. She would like to study

Graphic Arts and Interior Design.

She is a talented pianist.

Briana loves to dance and is learning to play the electric guitar and bass!

HOMESCHOOL YEARBOOK

Sports   Singing   Laughing   Sports   Singing

Kyla Rose Pierce
She is 13 years old here.
She loves all sports. She is very talented
At making other people laugh!
Kyla wants to be a singer!
She is also learning to play the electric guitar, bass & piano!

HOMESCHOOL YEARBOOK

Mark & Penni Pierce
A.K.A. Dad & Mom

*We have had a fun, exciting and sometimes scary
25 years together! We look forward to many more!*

Peace   Happiness   Love

HOMESCHOOL YEARBOOK

Then

1994-1995 School Year
Our First Year Homeschooling

Now

Briana, Rachel, Eric, Tahnee, Mark, Christy, Mark, Penni, Kyla